Apocalypse Encrypted!
Revelation Unleashed!

Part 2

By:

Anthony Montoya

Apocalypse Encrypted! Revelation Unleashed! Part 2

By

Anthony Montoya

Published By:

ABM Publications

A division of Andrew Bills Ministries Inc.

PO Box 6811, Orange, CA 92863

www.abmpublications.com

ISBN: 978-1-931820-57-8

DEDICATION

I would love to dedicate this book to my family & friends, who helped me through my walk of life. I would love to thank, David, Lupita, Nathaniel Sanchez & family, Pauli & Jack Taniguchi, My brothers Adrian Calderon and Robert Briseno for aiding me for shelter when I was living in my car. Also Prophet Mark, Sharon Sohmer, Mama McGee and Stevie. Prophetess Karen & Gilbert Bowser aiding me for shelter and food for several months. Prophetess Marie Santilliano for aiding me with intercession one night when I was in urgent need of a demonic attack, I was not supposed to be attending certain meetings where these spirits of warlocks and witches were even though they were apostles and prophets, I called Marie at midnight, I was being choked by a python spirit through a false prophet who astro projected out of his body and controlled another person to walk over to me and lay hands on me. She called it out within seconds and then rebuked me and corrected me. Prophetess Cynthia from Riverside California, Prophetess Cynthia from Glendale California. Prophetess Veronica from Rialto California, she called me one night while I was being attacked by the spirit of rejection & abandonment a dark heavy cloud, haven't spoke to her in three years and she called out of know where and broke the stronghold off me.

I would also like to thank, Prophetess Lily & Luis Avila, Sara, Denise, Prophet Brian & Claudia. Prophet Andre Hardin & Wife Pamela, Apostle Al Fornis for a major deliverance and breakthrough, Prophetess Deanne, Prophet Carlton LaGrange. Prophet Donnie from Louisiana who prophesied to me in detail and stated I had to wait 9 more months, and then I was removed from the burden of being homeless. Prophet Garret Lloyd, Prophet Michael Hodges & Family taking me through heavy healing and Deliverance. Prophet Hue Fortson taking me through heavy deliverance. Prophetess Stacy Yada, Apostle David Vizcara for aiding with money and material things. Prophet Alex & family, Prophetess Anita Morvac for her intercession, Prophetess Cindy from Upland California. Prophetess Young for her hospitality from Covina California. I would love to thank my brother Andrew from Corona California, Albert Garcia & family, Monique, Laura for aiding me food and money. Also I would love to thank Juan Valdez for shelter and food for several months. Prophet Evan walker for breaking a certain stronghold an affirming that it was over. My Parents Mary & Santiago for their tender loving care and hospitality.

SPECIAL APPRECIATION

I personally want to thank Bruce Dills and wife Shirley when I was homeless for shelter, food and aid. I also want to thank Gabriel Avila for his generous support funding Gods Kingdom, May Yeshua Increase and enlarge his Territory an End Time Prophet. I would also love to thank Ray Glory Ministries Prophetess Lilly Avila and Husband Prophet Mr. Burns. I would also love to thank Apostle Claudia and Prophet Brian Guerrero for making this happen, all their love and support. I would also love to Thank Apostle Sara Guerrero for her support and divine love and encouragement, a divine intercessor. I would also love to thank My Parents Mary & Santiago for all their hard work in everything they do. I would also love to thank my Publisher Andrew Bills and Family for His support.

TABLE OF CONTENTS

ACKNOWLEDGEMENTS

It is with much excitement and honor that I get the opportunity to acquaint you with my friend Anthony Montoya. In his unique style he reflects authentic leadership, tempered by a deep compassion for the lost. In this age of religious phonies and spiritual apathy, Anthony does not compromise the unfailing word of God.

His passion and exuberance for God is infectious; Challenging Christians to draw closer to God and take the Bible serious. During a time I was seeking a speaker for my Ministry, God said to me "call Anthony". God used Anthony to confirm some important future Ministry events that He had already spoken to me about. For the reasons above, and others that followed, I look forward to future Ministry with Anthony where his gifts will edify and be a blessing to the Body of Christ.

Lilly Avila
Rays of Glory Ministries, Inc.

In all the 19 years that I have known Anthony Montoya, he has been very poised and consistent. He's a man I know who rightly divides the Word of truth. He carefully hears from the Holy Spirit and he speaks as the Spirit gives him the utterance. I highly recommend his work to any reader out there.

Lloyd Nsek
Author of *"Christianity the End of Spiritual Confusion"*

CHAPTER 1

Saints this message is a Continuing from Book 3, what's on the bottom of the Menorah have on them, they have Almonds buds, which means the The Great I am, their eyes that can see. Those who have the Likeness of the Father, so who are the Cheri bums the eyes that can see on all sides (us). The almond tree has special significance, the name in Hebrew shakied, which comes from the root that means to watch or wake. Jeremiah 1 ^{11} Moreover the word of the LORD came unto me, saying, Jeremiah, what seest thou? And I said, I see a rod of an almond tree.^{12} Then said the LORD unto me, Thou hast well seen: for I will hasten my word to perform it. This mystery continues to be prepared for the 1,000 year reign here and now.

John 6:50-51 "This is the bread which comes down from heaven, that one may eat of it and not die. I am the living bread which came down from heaven. If anyone eats of this bread, he will live forever; and the bread that I shall give is My flesh, which I shall give for the life of the world."

Messenger in Greek means Angel, Matthew 11:10 for this is *he*, of whom it is written, Behold, I send my messenger before thy face, which shall prepare thy way before thee. He called John an angel, what do angels eat bread of Heaven supernatural truth of revelation. We are considered the Angels of Yahweh, Revelation 2:17 He that hath an ear, let him hear what the Spirit saith unto the churches; To him that overcometh will I give to eat of the hidden manna, and will give him a white stone, and in the stone a new name written, which no man knoweth saving he that receiveth it. The hidden word, the hidden Gospel (The good news) hidden from religion.

Exodus 25:16 "And you shall put into the ark the Testimony which I will give you." So who becomes the Ark that was in the Tabernacle it's us, we come in and will be in the same likeness as Yeshua walked the earth, the new Eon Age.

Hebrews 12:1 Wherefore seeing we also are compassed about with so great a cloud of witnesses, let us lay aside every weight, and the sin which doth so easily beset *us*, and let us run with patience the race that is set before us. Witness in Hebrew means Testimony hello! Who are the Testimonies us we shall be placed in the Ark which the Ark was placed in the Tabernacle where the Holy Holies resides in. We are the Tabernacle and the temple of the Holy Spirit.

Let's move on Saints, The bible states again he reveals his secrets and mysteries to his Holy Apostles & Prophets. Exodus 16 [16] This is the thing which the LORD hath commanded, Gather of it every man according to his eating, an omer for every man, according to the number of your persons; take ye every man for them which are in his tents. Omer means the binding of sheaf, this symbolic as the wheat and the tares. This symbolic means In Hebrew you have a people that have bitterness or twisted teachings of his word and those who do see and hear the truth and receive it. [17] And the children of Israel did so, and gathered some more, some less. [18] And when they did mete it with an omer, he that gathered much had nothing over, and he that gathered little had no lack; they gathered

4

every man according to his eating. Man in Hebrew means, wicked, sick, incurable, desperate, man of morality.

Jeremiah 17:9 [9] The heart is deceitful above all things, and desperately wicked: who can know it? You notice Eyeh Asher Eyeh was given man angels food, are angels sick, are angels mortal or immortal. So he gives us food that he gives Immortal beings.

Exodus 16: [19] And Moses said, Let no man leave of it till the morning. Do not leave any manna unturned eat of it all.[20] Notwithstanding they hearkened not unto Moses; but some of them left of it until the morning, and it bred worms (Bred in Hebrew means to lift oneself up, also means rotten maggot), and stank: and Moses was angry with them. This symbolic understanding is giving us precise instructions about old revelation or old manna just like the move of the Azusa street revival 100 years ago and churches are building up there camps around that teaching is considered maggot food. Yes we all have learned what transpired of such prophetic movements to grow I understand but we need to progress to hear what the spirit is saying today and what be caught up and catch up.

1 Corinthians 3 [11] For other foundation can no man lay than that is laid, which is Jesus Christ.[12] Now if any man build upon this foundation gold, silver, precious stones, wood, hay, stubble; [13] Every man's work shall be made manifest: for the day shall declare it, because it shall be revealed by fire; and the fire shall try every man's work of what sort it is.[14] If any man's work abide which he hath built thereupon, he shall receive a reward.[15] If any man's

work shall be burned, he shall suffer loss: but he himself shall be saved; yet so as by fire. What is wood considered twisted false teachings that will burn.

That means when you cling onto the same stuff or old teachings and you except compromise or complacency your maggot wormwood, maggots only cling to dead things. The verse continues to say (and Stank) Exodus 16:20, Revelation 3:17 Because thou sayest, I am rich, and increased with goods, and have need of nothing; and knowest not that thou art wretched, and miserable, and poor, and blind, and naked. Wretched you stink, why because you're filled with old teachings and twisted teachings and have no clue what's happening right now in the spirit.

Your power has grown weary. It goes on to say Moses was angry with them. The word angry in Hebrew means the snapping of a branch of wood, which is the Spirit of Abbadon. In the book of the Bible when Paul taught all night it was raining revelations no man or ear has heard or seen that's why it went so long.

Acts 20:9 Seated in a window was a young man named Eutychus, who was sinking into a deep sleep as Paul talked on and on. When he was sound asleep, he fell to the ground from the third story and was picked up dead. When you begin to fall asleep and not learn of his new revelations and his move of the spirit you will find yourself old and begin to decay, physically and spiritually. The father is also stating we can be broken off because we are not eating of the revelation. You notice Paul the Apostle states, 10 But Paul went down and bent over him and embraced him, saying, Make no ado; his life is within him.11 When Paul had gone back upstairs and had broken bread and eaten [with them], and after he had talked confidentially *and* communed with them for a considerable time—until daybreak [in fact]—he departed. 12 They took the youth home alive, and were not a little comforted *and* cheered *and* refreshed *and* encouraged. Paul the Apostle was filled with so much revelation he continued to minister, also the boy had so much meat of life within him, Paul had life given power to resurrect the dead in the midst of others. You also notice they took communion again to continue.

Exodus 16:21 And they gathered it every morning, every man according to his eating: and when the sun waxed hot, it melted.^{22} And it came to pass, that on the sixth day they gathered twice as much bread, two omers for one man: and all the rulers of the congregation came and told Moses. On the six day, they gathered twice as much bread, God rest on the 7th day in the book of Genesis, so the double portion of what we eat now there is no coming back to what you miss when the next move comes. Theirs is a new Ark floating or maneuvering around in the spirit and natural, so when the door closes that's it. You notice on the six day they gathered twice of much manna, double portion of meat. The time since Christ died on the cross this manna lasted 2,000 years. Doesn't the bible state Luke 4, Yeshua said this are the things which I have spoken to you about and the Law of Moses and the prophet also the book of Psalms concerning me? Law in Hebrew means Torah, Teachings, Prophets speak mysteries and secrets.

^{24} And they laid it up till the morning, as Moses bade: and it did not stink, neither was there any worm therein.^{25} And Moses said, Eat that today; for today is a Sabbath unto

7

the LORD: today ye shall not find it in the field.²⁶ Six days
ye shall gather it; but on the seventh day, which is the
Sabbath, in it there shall be none.²⁷ And it came to pass,
that there went out some of the people on the seventh day
for to gather, and they found none. The father stated eat
up what you can now of my double portion, of my manna
for it shall sustain you for the next 1,000 years. The six day
was double portion, the day the father rested, when the
next move in the tabernacle age and kingdom age and
does not eat to the secrets and mysteries and receive the
prophetic truth, when you go out in the field it will be dry
and dead, you shall find none.

**Num 17:7-8 "And Moses placed the rods before the LORD
in the tabernacle of witness. Now it came to pass on the
next day that Moses went into the tabernacle of witness,
and behold, the rod of Aaron, of the house of Levi, had
sprouted and put forth buds, had produced blossoms and
yielded ripe almonds."** So who then becomes the Rod, we
become the Rod, having the same spiritual universal power
as Yeshua, Psalms 2:9 Thou shalt break them with a rod of
iron; thou shalt dash them in pieces like a potter's vessel.
Revelation 2:27 And he shall rule them with a rod of iron;
as the vessels of a potter shall they be broken to shivers:
even as I received of my Father.

This is for those who get the revelation and those who
reject it. And he shall rule them with a rod of iron; as the
vessels of a potter shall they be broken to shivers: even as I
received of my Father. And he shall rule them with a rod of
iron; as the vessels of a potter shall they be broken to
shivers: even as I received of my Father.

Saints let's move on Exodus 16: 34 As the LORD commanded Moses, so Aaron laid it up before the Testimony, to be kept.35 And the children of Israel did eat manna forty years, until they came to a land inhabited; they did eat manna, until they came unto the borders of the land of Canaan.36 Now an omer is the tenth part of an ephah. Now in my previous book, manna is angel food, secrets and mysteries, you notice they came to a land called Canaan, What was in Canaan Giants, The nephilims the fallen angels. We are eating Angel's food preparing us to enter into a battle against the General demons of the city and nations. A battle against the fallen angels we need, descriptive precise functions and accuracy of the Holy Spirit for this next new move of Eyeh Asher Eyeh.

.

CHAPTER 2

The transfiguration of the new glorified body comes from the mind first, meaning eating of the Prophets and Apostles secrets from the Holy Spirit, to get this immortality. The father states he chastises and disciplines us correct, either with love or whip. Now what does whip mean to you, the rod, a spanking, OK and also when you whip something together its pressed or mixed with force. Sometimes the father needs to feed you manna or force you to eat it and shove it down your throat to eat it.

Psalms 78:22 Because they believed not in God, and trusted not in his salvation,23 Though he had commanded the clouds from above, and opened the doors of heaven,24 And had rained down manna upon them to eat, and had given them of the corn of heaven.25 Man did eat angels' food: he sent them meat to the full.

Matthew 4:3 And when the tempter came to him, he said, If thou be the Son of God, command that these stones be made bread.4 But he answered and said, It is written, Man shall not live by bread alone, but by every word that proceedeth out of the mouth of God. He wanted the stones to become word, what kind of word basic doctrine, religious carnal milk. Satan tried to get into even the very word of the bible we read. What is the resemblance of a stone, a rock, Matthew 16:18 And I say also unto thee, that thou art Peter, and upon this rock I will build my church; and the gates of hell shall not prevail against it. Rock resembles manna food, angel's food, also Apostles and Prophets feed you revelation and secrets and mysteries of the Kingdom. You shall not live just by regular sound doctrine of his word but manna that comes from Eyeh Asher Eyeh mouth, face to face.

Stone in Hebrew means eben (diverse weights) Yeshua says put on thy yoke for my burden is light, means learn of me. You notice in Deuteronomy 8:2 And thou shalt remember all the way which the LORD thy God led thee these forty years in the wilderness, to humble thee, and to prove thee, to know what was in thine heart, whether thou wouldst keep his commandments, or no.3 And he humbled thee, and suffered thee to hunger, and fed thee with manna, which thou newest not, neither did thy fathers know; that he might make thee know that man doth not live by bread only, but by every word that proceeding out of the mouth of the LORD doth man live. What is being impregnated in this revelation, Eyeyh Asher Eyeh said he feeds us secrets and mysteries from thy Apostles and Prophets, but also this manna did they not know nor did their fathers new, this Manna is from Yahweh's mouth, face to face mouth to mouth.

Amos chap 3:7 Surely the Lord GOD will do nothing, but he revealeth his secret unto his servants the prophets. Ephesians 3:3 How that by revelation he made known unto me the mystery; (as I wrote a fore in few words, 4 whereby, when ye read, ye may understand my knowledge in the mystery of Christ) 5 Which in other ages was not made known unto the sons of men, as it is now revealed unto his holy apostles and prophets by the Spirit; Satan tried to make Yeshua eat natural revelation of Eyeh Asher Eyeh word, John: 6 30 They said therefore unto him, what sign shewest thou then, that we may see, and believe thee? What dost thou work? 31 Our fathers did eat manna in the desert; as it is written, He gave them bread from heaven to eat. 32 Then Jesus said unto them, Verily, verily, I say unto you, Moses gave you not that bread from heaven; but my Father giveth you the true bread from heaven.33 For the bread of God is he which comet h down from heaven, and giveth life unto the world.34 Then said they unto him, Lord, evermore give us this bread. You notice he was speaking from a different form of bread that comes from Eyeh Asher Eyeh mouth.

John 6: 35 And Jesus said unto them, I am the bread of life: he that cometh to me shall never hunger; and he that believeth in me shall never thirst (never hunger or thirsts for what? Revelation).36 But I said unto you, That ye also have seen me, and believe not.37 All that the Father giveth me shall come to me; and him that cometh to me I will in no wise cast out.38 For I came down from heaven, not to do mine own will, but the will of him that sent me.39 And this is the Father's will which hath sent me, that of all which he hath given me I should lose nothing, but should raise it up again at the last day. At the end of the age I am going to raise everything up. They wanted something in the supernatural to come down from heaven. Maybe some sort of superman figure like combo, he did but in words of his teachings which were natural but supernatural. 40 And this is the will of him that sent me, that everyone which seethe the Son, and believeth on him, may have everlasting life: and I will raise him up at the last day.

41 The Jews then murmured at him, because he said, I am the bread which came down from heaven. What were they murmuring about, or complaining about the manna the way it was being presented to them just like you and I in the church rejecting the Apostles and Prophets when anything comes against their money and control of the

people and their salary cap, or there twisted teachings and false doctrine and the Tithe.

42 And they said, is not this Jesus, the son of Joseph, whose father and mother we know? How is it then that he saith, I came down from heaven? 43 Jesus therefore answered and said unto them, Murmur not among yourselves.

Just like they murmured with Moses in the wilderness for forty years. 44 No man can come to me, except the Father which hath sent me draw him: and I will raise him up at the last day.45 It is written in the prophets, and they shall be all taught of God. Every man therefore that hath heard, and hath learned of the Father, cometh unto me.46 Not that any man hath seen the Father, save he which is of God, he hath seen the Father.47 Verily, verily, I say unto you, He that believeth on me hath everlasting life.48 I am that bread of life.49 Your fathers did eat manna in the wilderness, and are dead.

Continued 50 This is the bread which cometh down from heaven, that a man may eat thereof, and not die (Hello Immortality).51 I am the living bread which came down from heaven: if any man eat of this bread, he shall live forever: and the bread that I will give is my flesh, which I will give for the life of the world.52 The Jews therefore strove among themselves, saying, How can this man give us his flesh to eat? 53 Then Jesus said unto them, Verily, verily, I say unto you, except ye eat the flesh of the Son of man, and drink his blood, ye have no life in you. Unless you Eat the Mysteries of the Kingdom, you have no life in you for this next move, Pentecost last 2,000 years from Acts, theirs a new form of revelation manna food here and now.

Matthew 24: 3 And as he sat upon the Mount of Olives, the disciples came unto him privately, saying, Tell us, when shall these things be? And what shall be the sign of thy coming, and of the end of the world?

The end of the old age and the beginning of the new age, 10 and then shall many be offended, and shall betray one another, and shall hate one another. When they become offended stripping them of control over your mind, body soul and spirit, their money, their Tithe, there salary and their false teachings and false doctrine, they will be infuriated. The motive and intentions of their hearts will be laid bare out in the open.

Genesis 1:1 In the beginning God created the heaven and the earth.2 And the earth was without form, and void; and darkness was upon the face of the deep. And the Spirit of God moved upon the face of the waters.3 And God said, Let there be light: and there was light. So then Eyeh Asher Eyeh moves in the water which was symbolic of Holy Spirit but of revelation of his word. Deuteronomy said let my Revelation fall like the rain (water) upon this earth. Continued verse 14 And God said, Let there be lights in the firmament of the heaven to divide the day from the night; and let them be for signs, and for seasons, and for days, and years: this light had to be supernatural revelation first from his wisdom and understanding.

Firmament in Hebrew means to beat out, or waters above it, also ark of the sky, meaning Eyeh Asher Eyeh wants to burn out the firmaments of our minds. In my First and Second book as I explained mesocratic cells condition of memory bubbles in the mind. Hammer out to make everything level and straight, Proverbs state is not my word like a hammer, making it level straight and narrow. 2

Peter 3: But the day of the Lord will come as a thief in the night; in the heavens shall pass away with a great noise, and the elements shall melt with fervent heat, the earth also and the works that are therein shall be burned up.

Elements are firmaments of the sky, your mind and everything you built up, will be made bare in Hebrew means to be emptied, naked unclothed stripped of the false. Furthermore which means mind, body, soul and spirit.

Galatians 4:3 So also we, while we were children, were held in bondage under the elemental things of the world,: 9 But now that you have come to know God, or rather to be known by God, how is it that you turn back again to the weak and worthless elemental things, to which you desire to be enslaved all over again? Colossian 2:8 See to it that no one takes you captive through philosophy and empty deception, according to the tradition of men, according to the elementary principles of the world, rather than according to Christ. Hebrews 5:2 For though by this time you ought to be teachers, you have need again for someone to teach you the elementary principles of the oracles of God, and you have come to need milk and not solid food.

Psalms 104:2 Covering yourself with light as with a cloak, stretching out heaven like a tent curtain. - See. The false teachings that the earth is going to be destroyed by missiles and bombs etc. "And I will give power unto my two witnesses, and they shall prophesy a thousand two hundred and threescore days, clothed in sackcloth. *Revelation 11:3* The term "threescore" literally means three times 20 (which is a "score" in old English). So it actually means 1260 days. This means it is 3 1/2 years of

360 days (or a prophetic year) for each year. The prophets, Yeshua and Apostle have been prophesying for the last 3,5oo years from the time outer court (1500 cubits) Moses went to the Mountain to see Eyeh Asher Eyeh face to face Pentecost, the inner court (10x20x10=2,000) the church age since Yeshua died on the cross and Pentecost from the book Acts. We are entering the Holy of Holies The tabernacle age, Eon age.

Revelation 11: And I will give power unto my two witnesses, and they shall prophesy a thousand two hundred [and] threescore days, clothed in sackcloth. 4 These are the two olive trees, and the two candlesticks standing before the God of the earth. 5 And if any man will hurt them, fire proceedeth out of their mouth, and devoureth their enemies: and if any man will hurt them, he must in this manner be killed. 6 These have power to shut heaven, that it rain not in the days of their prophecy: and have power over waters to turn them to blood, and to smite the earth with all plagues, as often as they will. Moses and Elijah moved in this manner, two means a man or group of sectors, now man needs a spirit embodiment.

7 And when they shall have finished their testimony, the beast (those who bared the mark of the 666 and rejected the Apostolic mysteries) that ascendeth out of the bottomless pit shall make war against them, and shall overcome them, and kill them (Themselves). Moses was sent to be shut up, Eyeh Asher Eyeh told him go to the Mountain and die testimonies finished. The Testimony of the Prophetic message, to be shut up, just like John the Baptist (was beheaded), the word Elijah has come but did not recognize him.

8 And their dead bodies shall lie in the street of the great city, which spiritually is called Sodom and Egypt (Sodom is wickedness-Canaanite city the Nephilim's fallen angels) (Egypt double minded- double tongue), where also our Lord was crucified.9 And they of the people and kindreds and tongues and nations shall see their dead bodies three days and an half, and shall not suffer their dead bodies to be put in graves.

9 Matthew 14; 2 And said unto his servants, this is John the Baptist; he is risen from the dead; and therefore mighty works do shew forth themselves in him. Yeshua's body was place in a tomb, not a grave underneath the ground. Judah 1:9 Yet Michael the archangel, when contending with the devil he disputed about the body of Moses, durst not bring against him a railing accusation, but said, The Lord rebuke thee. Not even Moses body either, they were both overtaken. 11 And after three days and an half the spirit of life from God entered into them, and they stood upon their feet; and great fear fell upon them which saw them. The Spirit of Full Authority Full Dominion Immortality is given, universal power.

10 Saints you notice Jude 1:4 For there are certain men crept in unawares, who were before of old ordained to this condemnation, ungodly men, turning the grace of our God into lasciviousness, and denying the only Lord God, and our Lord Jesus Christ.5 I will therefore put you in remembrance, though ye once knew this, how that the Lord, having saved the people out of the land of Egypt, afterward destroyed them that believed not.6 And the angels which kept not their first estate (Nephilims, Fallen angels even Satan), but left their own habitation, he hath reserved in everlasting chains under darkness unto the

judgment of the great day.7 Even as Sodom (Giants, fallen angels) and Gomorrah, and the cities about them in like manner, giving themselves over to fornication, and going after strange flesh, are set forth for an example, suffering the vengeance of eternal fire.

11 8 Likewise also these filthy dreamers defile the flesh, despise dominion (mock the revelations and secrets), and speak evil of dignities. The false teachers, false prophets and fallen angels, 10 but these speak evil of those things which they know not: but what they know naturally, as brute beasts, in those things they corrupt themselves.11 Woe unto them! for they have gone in the way of Cain, and ran greedily after the error of Balaam for reward, and perished in the gainsaying of Core.12 These are spots in your feasts of charity(Plague is black spot), when they feast with you, feeding themselves without fear: clouds(false teachings) they are without water(No revelation or carry the Presence of Eyeh Asher Eyeh, carried about of winds(philosophy, fables false teachings); trees whose fruit withereth, without fruit, twice dead, plucked up by the(roots;13 Raging waves of the sea(without form of Christ) , foaming out their own shame; wandering stars(Great titles and names), to whom is reserved the blackness of darkness forever.

16 These are murmurers, complainers, walking after their own lusts; and their mouth speaketh great swelling words (Great conferences) , having men's persons in admiration because of advantage (Mens or Kingdom of this world them being admired cause of their upper hand or advantage they have).17 But, beloved, remember ye the words which were spoken before of the apostles of our Lord Jesus Christ; 18 How that they told you there should

be mockers in the last time, who should walk after their own ungodly lusts.19 These be they who separate themselves, sensual, having not the Spirit.

Now did it not specifically state, His Apostles and Prophets warned you and can only perceive this kind of counterfeit angel of light spirits. The answer to this is 20 But ye, beloved, building up yourselves on your most holy faith, praying in the Holy Ghost, the edification of speaking in an unknown tongue heavenly.

Revelation 11:12 And they heard a great voice from heaven saying unto them, Come up Hither (Transfigured into Immortality). And they ascended up to heaven in a cloud(received immortality form); and their enemies beheld them.13 And the same hour was there a great earthquake, and the tenth part of the city fell, and in the earthquake were slain of men seven thousand: and the remnant were frightened, and gave glory to the God of heaven.14 The second woe is past; and, behold, the third woe cometh quickly(3$^{rd.}$ day new age, 1,000 year reign) .15 And the seventh angel sounded; and there were great voices in heaven, saying, The kingdoms of this world (Earth) are become the kingdoms of our Lord, and of his Christ; and he shall reign for ever and ever. You notice it stated tenth, a portion of his remnant, then it states 7seven thousand were slain, the remnant were placed or transfigured into perfection.

17 Saying, We give thee thanks, O LORD God Almighty, which art, and wast, and art to come; because thou hast taken to thee thy great power, and hast reigned. He has taken to thee in Hebrew means (to bear fruit, those who

died to themselves and grew and increase in revelation and character).

18 And the nations were angry, and thy wrath is come, and the time of the dead, that they should be judged, and that thou shouldest give reward unto thy servants the prophets, and to the saints, and them that fear thy name, small and great; and shouldest destroy them which destroy the earth.19 And the temple of God was opened in heaven, and there was seen in his temple the ark of his testament: and there were lightnings, and voices, and thundering s, and an earthquake, and great hail. The temple, tabernacle the veils ripped open inside of us, the Ark of His testament of who the Father is Eyeh Asher Eyeh in and through us, lightning in Hebrew (bright glittering word) wine of revelation, thunderings in Hebrew shouting or stir, stirring of his universal bliss his power, Earthquake in Hebrew means trembling.

Jeremiah 33:9 And it shall be to me a name of joy, a praise and an honor before all the nations of the earth, which shall hear all the good that I do unto them: and they shall fear and tremble for all the goodness and for all the prosperity that I procure unto it. In Hebrew Hail means stones, which also means his bread, manna his word of revelation and it hailed revelations.

Matthew 22: And Jesus answered and spake unto them again by parables, and said,2 The kingdom of heaven is like unto a certain king, which made a marriage for his son,3 And sent forth his servants(Apostles and prophets) to call them that were bidden to the wedding(The church is invited to the wedding, the saints do not want to come, they rather pay teachers to tickle their ears and the religious systems): Again he sent forth his servants, 'Tell them that are bidden,' Behold(See get an understanding) I have prepared my dinner(Before my marriage takes place you need to eat manna revelation come to the end of yourselves),Hebrew thought the dinner takes place first before the wedding): my oxen(Apostles and Prophets are read they have died to themselves) and my fat-lings are killed, and all things are ready(The dinner is ready is been prepared): come unto the marriage.5 But they made light of it(the did not take it seriously), and went their ways, one to his farm(went to their own ministries and businesses), another to his merchandise(corporations businesses):6 And the remnant took his servants, and entreated them spitefully, and slew them. Apostles and prophets treated them with rudeness, mocked and laughed at them. Killed means they want you to shut up! It does not mean a natural death.

7 But when the king heard thereof he was wroth, and he sent forth his armies and destroyed those murderers (Eyeh Asher Eyeh destroyed the church carnal Christians) removal of the wicked the Christian-Abdominal swine flu, and burned up their city.8 Then said he to his servants, 'The wedding is ready, but they that were bidden were not worthy.9 Go ye therefore into the highways, and as many as ye shall find, bid to the marriage.

So those servants went out into the highways (those lead to destruction), and gathered all together as many as they found, both bad and good, and the wedding was furnished with guests.11 And when the king came in to see the guests, he saw there a man who did not have on a wedding garment.12 And he said unto him, 'Friend (Family we are friends in Eyeh Asher Eyeh army), how camest thou in hither not having a wedding garment?'(He is preparing our Wedding garment for Marriage) And he was speechless.13 Then said the king to the servants, 'Bind him hand and foot and take him away, and cast him into outer darkness: there shall be weeping and gnashing of teeth.' Meaning he is telling us this time there is no looking around on the 7th day for left over manna, once this is closed up its over, there will be weeping and gnashing of teeth. Outer darkness is not hell, it's a place with no revelation or life.

14 For many are called, but few (that understand and receive the hidden mysteries) are chosen."15 Then the Pharisees went and took counsel how they might entangle Him in His talk. Again trying to shut him up. Genesis 17:5 Neither shall thy name any more be called Abram, but thy name shall be Abraham; for a father of many nations have I made thee.6 And I will make thee exceeding fruitful, and I will make nations of thee, and kings shall come out of thee.7 And I will establish My covenant between Me and thee and thy seed after thee in their generations for an everlasting covenant, to be a God unto thee and to thy seed after thee.8 And I will give unto thee and to thy seed(Remnant of the 12 tribes all of his chosen vessels) after thee the land wherein thou art a stranger, all the land of Canaan, for an everlasting possession; and I will be their God." Part of the covenant of Abraham to his seed, the current Jews do they have Canaan land, Iraq, Syria, Egypt and Kuwait, they don't have not even 1%. The oil is the Jews oil, symbolic of the Holy Spirit, those who will inherit the fullness of the Spirit.

Genesis 17:14 And the uncircumcised man child whose flesh of his foreskin is not circumcised, that soul shall be cut off from his people; he hath broken My covenant."

When you do not die to yourself completely you are broken off or there is a divorce of a marriage agreement. Revelation 12:5 And she brought forth a man child, who was to rule all nations with a rod of iron: and her child was caught up unto God, and to his throne.

6 And the woman fled into the wilderness, where she hath a place prepared of God, that they should feed her there a thousand two hundred and threescore days. That number 1,290 days a time, times and a half of time, 3 ½, which resembles 3,500. The outer court 1,500 cubits, inner court 10x20x10=2000 years. This food last 3,500 years until now, Moses days and now church age since the day Yeshua reigned and resurrected 2,000 years.

Genesis 17:19 And God said, "Sarah thy wife shall bear thee a son indeed, and thou shalt call his name Isaac; and I will establish My covenant with him for an everlasting covenant, and with his seed after him.20 And as for Ishmael, I have heard thee. Behold, I have blessed him, and will make him fruitful and will multiply him exceedingly. Twelve princes shall he beget, and I will make him a great nation. I will make all my descendants the 12 tribes of Israel prosperous. Isaac in Hebrew means Yaqoob (A supplanter takes the place of someone or something that was there first. For example, a new big-name donut shop may become a supplanter if it hurts or ruins the business of the local Mom and Pop donut shop.

Supplanter often refers to governments and rulers of countries, and it comes from the verb *supplant*, which evolved from the Latin *supplantare*, meaning "to trip up or to overthrow." You do not become a Prince until you receive universal power.

CHAPTER 3

Revelation 12:10 And I heard a loud voice saying in heaven, Now is come salvation, and strength, and the kingdom of our God, and the power of his Christ: for the accuser of our brethren is cast down, which accused them before our God day and night.

11 And they overcame him by the blood of the Lamb, and by the word of their testimony; and they loved not their lives unto the death. The remnant died to themselves completely.

12 Therefore rejoice, ye heavens, and ye that dwell in them. Woe to the inhabitants of the earth and of the sea! For the devil is come down unto you, having great wrath, because he knoweth that he hath but a short time.

13 And when the dragon saw that he was cast unto the earth, he persecuted the woman which brought forth the man child. The church has been under persecution for the last 3,500 years.

14 And to the woman were given two wings of a great eagle, that she might fly into the wilderness, into her place, where she is nourished for a time, and times, and half a time, from the face of the serpent.

The place of heights and understanding no matter what it looks like the body of Christ the church is the woman. Isaiah 40:31 But those who wait for the Lord [who expect, look for, and hope in Him] shall change *and* renew their strength *and* power; they shall lift their wings *and* mount up [close to God] as eagles [mount up to the sun]; they shall run and not be weary, they shall walk and not faint *or* become tired.

15 And the serpent cast out of his mouth water as a flood after the woman, that he might cause her to be carried away of the flood. Isaiah 59:19 So shall they fear the name of the LORD from the west and His glory from the rising of the sun. When the enemy shall come in like a flood, the Spirit of the LORD shall lift up a standard against him.

16 And the earth helped the woman, and the earth opened her mouth, and swallowed up the flood which the dragon cast out of his mouth. Earth in Hebrew means to be firm, grounded in his word.

17 And the dragon was wroth with the woman, and went to make war with the remnant of her seed, which keep the commandments of God, and have the testimony of Jesus Christ. Satan or dragon the spirit of Abbadon, Appolyn has been fighting the church last 3,500 years. Isaiah 59:21 "As for me, this is my covenant with them," saith the LORD; "My spirit that is upon thee, and My words which I have put in thy mouth, shall not depart out of thy mouth, nor out of the mouth of thy seed, nor out of the mouth of thy seed's seed," saith the LORD, "from henceforth and forever." My seed which I plant shall not return or come unto me void, but shall continue forever and ever Eons.

Isaiah 55:11 So shall my word be that goeth forth out of my mouth: it shall not return unto me void, but it shall accomplish that which I please, and it shall prosper *in the thing* whereto I sent it. My seeds shall not come back to me emptied handed until we attain and retain all of the Earths Wealth, all of it and rule and come back hand over to the father the Conquered Earth, then Yeshua will come back.

Revelation 12:1 And there appeared a great wonder in heaven; a woman clothed with the sun(The church Clothed in the same likeness and form of Yeshua in his body form Immortality), and the moon under her feet(Moon in Hebrew means yereach-Permanence) the state or quality of lasting or remaining unchanged indefinitely(stability, durability, permanency, fixity, fixedness, changeless, immutability, endurance, constancy, continuity, immortality, indestructibility, perpetuity, endlessness "the permanence of their relationship gives them a mutual sense of security" , and upon her head a crown of twelve stars: The 12 tribes of Israel, the remnant Star in Hebrew means Prince, You are not a Prince unto you have been given Universal Power! Like your Daddy the Creator and Ownership of all things, they shall inherit all things of Heaven and on Earth.

Psalms 89:1-29 Read for yourselves, you notice verse, 11 the heavens are Thine, the earth also is Thine; as for the world and the fullness thereof, Thou hast founded them. 22 The enemy shall not exact from him, nor the son of wickedness afflict him. 23 And I will beat down his foes before his face, and plague them that hate him. 27 Also I will make him My firstborn, higher than the kings of the earth.

Romans 2:24 For, "The name of God is blasphemed among the Gentiles through you," as it is written.25 For circumcision verily profiteth if thou keep the law; but if thou be a breaker of the law, thy circumcision is made uncircumcised.26 Therefore if the Uncircumcised keep the righteousness of the law, shall not his uncircumcision be counted for circumcision? 27 And shall not uncircumcision, which is by nature, if it fulfill the law, judge thee, who having the letter and circumcision dost transgress the law? 28 For he is not a Jew who is one outwardly, neither is that circumcision, which is outward in the flesh.29 But he is a Jew who is one inwardly, and whose circumcision is that of the heart, in the spirit and not in the letter, and whose praise is not from men, but from God.

The father Eyeh Asher Eyeh specifically states just because you understand the dead letter of the law which is the word you're not circumcised yet. Once you die completely to yourself and circumcise your heart, and with the Leading of the Holy spirit not just the milk of the word. It states only the Holy Spirit of purified understanding from the spirit not just the letter of the word that your reading does the job.

Roman 4:8 blessed is the man to whom the Lord will not impute sin."9 Cometh this blessedness then upon the Circumcision only, or upon the Uncircumcised also? For we say that faith was reckoned to Abraham for righteousness.10 How was it then reckoned? When he was in circumcision, or in uncircumcision? Not in circumcision, but in uncircumcision! Saints faith in Hebrew means (agreement) Circumcision is a purified understanding of the word by the spirit. Abraham received Eyeh Asher Eyeh blessing as a natural man, that's what uncircumcised meant. So you only receive a circumcision by when you agree with his spirit and by the True Apostle and Prophets manna. Also Abraham received a circumcision by revelation of his word by spirit. Abraham agreed with the will and instructions of Eye Ashe Eye and received the revelation that was given to him and then only then he was counted as righteous. So every time you get revelation which is a purified understanding, it's a revelation.

Saints OK you're asking yourself some minute questions, then why in no matter what religion is pronounced out there and people act the same or have a Dr. Jeckle and Dr. Hyde spirit or character. It is because they never received a revelation of what was feed to them by the simplified doctrine dead letter of the law. Hebrew 10:20 by a new and living Way, which He hath consecrated for us through the veil (that is to say, His flesh), Saints revelation means opening of the veils, so when you receive a revelation, your flesh is being removed off of your heart, that means your been circumcised in your heart!

Romans 4:11 And he received the sign of circumcision, a seal of the righteousness of the faith which he had, yet being uncircumcised, that he might be the father of all those who believe, though they are not circumcised, that righteousness might be imputed unto them also, 12 and the father of circumcision to those who are not of the Circumcision only, but who also walk in the steps of that faith of our father Abraham which he had, being yet uncircumcised. The seal of righteousness is to have a right understanding, righteousness in Hebrew means in (conduct and character), but also means a rightful understanding of revelation. So believers worldwide because you believe and study the dead letter of the law and obey its laws and regulations of legalisms like Tithing, going to church one a week and never receive a revelation of the Torah (Word) how can you be saved, if you never received a revelation or had your heart circumcised by the Holy spirit with the word.

Psalms 1: [Psalm *1]* Blessed *is* the man that walketh not in the counsel of the ungodly, nor standeth in the way of sinners, nor sitteth in the seat of the scornful. But his delight *is* in the law of the Lord; and in his law doth he meditate day and night. And he shall be like a tree planted by the rivers of water, that bringeth forth his fruit in his season; his leaf also shall not wither; and whatsoever he doeth shall prosper. . The law is (Torah his word), his revelations and get a purified understanding of it and then receive a circumcision within the heart while your indwelling with it or having intercourse with it.

Romans 13:8 Owe no man anything, but to love one another, for he that loveth another hath fulfilled the law, you notice it states only when you have true love for one another, you have fulfilled the (Torah Word)when you fall in love with his revelations to receive a circumcised heart.9 For this, "Thou shalt not commit adultery," "Thou shalt not kill," "Thou shalt not steal," "Thou shalt not bear false witness," "Thou shalt not covet," and if there be any other commandment, all are briefly comprehended in this saying, namely: "Thou shalt love thy neighbor as thyself."10 Love worketh no ill to his neighbor; therefore love is the fulfillment of the law.11 And that, knowing the time, that now it is high time to awaken out of sleep; for now is our salvation nearer than when we first believed.12 The night is far spent; the day is at hand. Let us therefore cast off the works of darkness, and let us put on the armor of light.13

Let us walk honestly as in the day, not in rioting and drunkenness, not in lewdness and wantonness, not in strife and envying.14 But put ye on the Lord Jesus Christ, and make not provision for the flesh to fulfill the lusts thereof.

Sleep in Hebrew means (Lack, lack of understanding and revelation) it also means to die. Ask yourself are you coming into deeper love of his character, conduct, revelations of his word. Darkness means the dead letter of the law the word, Armor of Light, the revelation of his word. Rioting in Greek means living in sensual, lustful behavior. Drunkenness in Hebrew means to be intoxicated or influenced, polluted with false doctrine and to be polluted with influential spirits very easily. Lewdness in Hebrew means to plan out purposely deceitfulness and wickedness. Wantonness in Hebrew means to practice evil deeds.

Jeremiah 4:4 Circumcise yourselves to the LORD, and take away the foreskins of your heart, ye men of Judah and inhabitants of Jerusalem, lest My fury come forth like fire, and burn that none can quench it, because of the evil of your doings. The fire is not a natural fire, it is the Revelation of the Torah, The two witnesses in the book of Revelation speaks of they shall Prophesy, they shall speak like fire! This new fire of revelation it will burn and no one can shut it up or take it out. The destruction of Fury is not the fire to destroy the world, it is to destroy the wickedness and evil in your heart to burn it out! That is His Love and Eyeh Asher Eyeh the Daddy we serve.

Lamentations 3:62 The lips *and* thoughts of my assailants are against me all day long.63 Look at their sitting down and their rising up [their movements, doings, and secret counsels]; I am their singsong [the subject of their derision and merriment].64 Render to them a recompense, O Lord, according to the work of their hands.65 You will give them hardness *and* blindness of heart(veiled heart); Your curse will be upon them.66 You will pursue *and* afflict them in anger and destroy them from under Your heavens, O Lord. If your heart if veiled and have no revelation of understanding of his truth of the word prophetically your cursed. The reasoning's and understandings of yourselves have strong spiritual demons come out of you when you're veiled.

Nicodemus asked Jesus Christ what must I do to become born again, did Jesus tell him to kneel down and pray this prayer, no he said John 3;3 Jesus answered and said unto him, "Verily, verily I say unto thee, unless a man be born again, he cannot see the Kingdom of God." This meant to be Resurrected in heart body mind soul and spirit. The answer is repent of your sins no matter what, but he wanted him to understand his word of understanding within internally.

4 Nicodemus said unto Him, "How can a man be born when he is old? Can he enter a second time into his mother's womb and be born?"5 Jesus answered, "Verily, verily I say unto thee, unless a man be born of water and of the Spirit, he cannot enter into the Kingdom of God.6 That which is born of the flesh is flesh; and that which is born of the Spirit is spirit. You cannot be of Carnality or carnal understanding, you must receive and be willing to have your heart circumcised by the spirit through his word.

Saints so going to church, paying Tithes (Law) not scriptural, and reading the dead letter of the law, with no water and no spirit and no heart being circumcised are you really saved. Jeremiah 11: The LORD gave another message to Jeremiah. He said, 2 "Remind the people of Judah and Jerusalem about the terms of my covenant with them. 3 Say to them, 'This is what the LORD, the God of Israel, says: Cursed is anyone who does not obey the terms of my covenant! 4 For I said to your ancestors when I brought them out of the iron-smelting furnace of Egypt, "If you obey me and do whatever I command you, then you will be my people, and I will be your God." 5 I said this so I could keep my promise to your ancestors to give you a land flowing with milk and honey—the land you live in today.' "Then I replied, "Amen, LORD! May it be so."

6 Then the LORD said, "Broadcast this message in the streets of Jerusalem. Go from town to town throughout the land and say, 'Remember the ancient covenant, and do everything it requires. 7 For I solemnly warned your ancestors when I brought them out of Egypt, "Obey me!" I have repeated this warning over and over to this day, 8 but your ancestors did not listen or even pay attention. Instead, they stubbornly followed their own evil desires. And because they refused to obey, I brought upon them all the curses described in this covenant.'"

When his Apostles and Prophets, are shut up and disregard their teachings and messages from their mouths, which is the Ark of the Covenant, had two angels, one side the other side one, one wing left side one wing right side, put them together resembles the mouth. This means your breaking covenant with Eyeh Asher Eyeh, so when all religions reject the Apostles and Prophets they become cursed. Well some you say how when many are living luxurious and wealthy, yes you are correct, doesn't it state that Eyeh Asher Eyeh will hardened their hearts and blind them from the truth. That is even a more freighting experience you don't want to tap into.

Matthew 27: 50 And Jesus cried again with a loud voice, and yielded up his spirit.51 And behold, the veil of the temple was rent in two from the top to the bottom; and the earth did quake; and the rocks were rent;52 and the tombs were opened; and many bodies of the saints that had fallen asleep were raised;53 and coming forth out of the tombs after his resurrection they entered into the holy city and appeared unto many.54 Now the centurion, and they that were with him watching Jesus, when they saw the earthquake, and the things that were done, feared exceedingly, saying, Truly this was the Son of God.

The veil the secrets and mysteries of what he spoke of, was water and spirit, they pierced his side water came out, and yielded up his spirit, he stop talking, the earth shook, people trembled, the rocks were split the bread was broken in half, his word of his spirit, the ones that were asleep were raised from their tombs after his resurrection. It was so powerful meaning many were asleep to his teachings and all of a sudden they became alive and understood what he was speaking of. Something entered their spirit so profoundly a revelation hit them with understanding they said truly he was the Son of Yahweh.

Philippians 3:10 That I may know him, and the power of his resurrection, and the fellowship of his sufferings, being made conformable unto his death. When he can understand the seed of his word through revelations, and have nothing offend him through sufferings, dying completely to self. Then I will know him and his power of

Resurrection. I do believe that you can have and receive a circumcision of the heart through experiences even if you can't understand the word of Yahweh. Worship does bring deliverance, in my walk my favorite two scriptures were (Create in me a clean heart O father and renew a right spirit within me), that was in the book of Psalms, also book of Ephesians, Grant unto me the spirit of wisdom revelation and understanding. Saints do not be Discouraged if someone tells you, just because you speak in tongues and worship and dance and you don't understand his revelations you're not saved.

That is not all correct, speaking in tongues is a secret and mystery and an answer, worship is the key also. I will prove it to you.

1 Corinthians 14:2 For he that speaketh in an *unknown* tongue speaketh not unto men, but unto God: for no man understandeth *him*; howbeit in the spirit he speaketh mysteries. Yes is specifically states mysteries which means unknown revelations. The book of Jude speaks about beware of seducing spirits and teachings, and it states to pray in your most (Holy faith). Faith in Hebrew means also covenant, when you agree with the spirit you're accepting his covenant, edification of speaking in tongues. Psalms 32:7 Thou *art* my hiding place; thou shalt preserve me from trouble; thou shalt compass me about with songs of deliverance. Worship is the ultimate answer and key to Deliverance and a circumcised heart. This will help you to understand and receive a transfiguration to die to yourself completely and understand his ways. When He Yahweh means worship it means with all your heart mind body soul and strength. That means with all exhaustion, not just breaking a little sweat, which none of us possibly do

35

anyway during worship in a service, it means to be drenched in sweat, to be clothed with water pouring out.

Numbers 12: And Miriam and Aaron spoke against Moses because of the Ethiopian woman whom he had married, for he had married an Ethiopian woman.2 And they said, "Hath the LORD indeed spoken only by Moses? Hath He not spoken also by us?" And the LORD heard it. 4 And the LORD spoke suddenly unto Moses and unto Aaron and unto Miriam: "Come out ye three unto the tabernacle of the congregation." And the three came out.5 And the LORD came down in the pillar of the cloud and stood in the door of the tabernacle, and called Aaron and Miriam; and they both came forth.6 And He said, "Hear now My words: If there be a prophet among you, I, the LORD, will make Myself known unto him in a vision, and will speak unto him in a dream.7 My servant Moses is not so, who is faithful in all Mine house.8 With him will I speak mouth to mouth, even plainly, and not in dark speeches; and the similitude of the LORD shall he behold. Why then were ye not afraid to speak against My servant Moses?"

You notice the Father is speaking to Levels of Prophets, Outer court is the dream and vision center, the inner court is the parables and symbolism stage(Menorah the gifts and talents the church Apostolic), then you have the Holy of Holies stage, face to face ,mouth to mouth secrets and mysteries defined ac accurately(Holy Apostles and Prophets). You notice Aaron and Miriam spoke and stated has not Yahweh spoken to us also. Saints you notice Yahweh stated those prophets and apostles I speak through a dream or vision, then those I speak through parables and symbolism's, then those who Speak secrets and Mysteries Face to Face! Ezekiel 17:2And the word of the LORD came unto me, saying, 2 "Son of man, put forth a riddle, and speak a parable unto the house of Israel. There is a process through manifolds of interpretation, this is considered a parable or proverb and a riddle.

You notice the father speaks to certain Prophets plainly and not in dark speech, this is a favorable grace and merciful given experience. 9 And the anger of the LORD was kindled against them, and He departed.10 And the cloud departed from off the tabernacle. And behold, Miriam became leprous, white as snow; and Aaron looked upon Miriam, and behold, she was leprous. Those who speak up against those who speak face to face with Daddy is not a good thing. You notice there is another revelation of inclusion to this mystery. This inspiration even give counter effects to those who are true intercessors. Saints gossip isn't good at all, but it gives even to say do not speak up against intercessors also who hear his word Face to Face!

Luke 10:38 Now it came to pass, as they went, that He entered into a certain village; and a certain woman named Martha received Him into her house.39 And she had a sister called Mary, who also sat at Jesus' feet and heard His Word.40 But Martha was encumbered with much serving, and came to Him and said, "Lord, dost Thou not care that my sister hath left me to serve alone? Bid her therefore that she help me."41 And Jesus answered and said unto her, "Martha, Martha, thou art anxious and troubled about many things.42 But one thing is needful, and Mary hath chosen that good part, which shall not be taken away from her."

Saints let's move on, Seventy has a sacred meaning in the Bible that is made up of the factors of two perfect numbers, seven (representing perfection) and ten (representing completeness and God's law). As such, it symbolizes perfect spiritual order carried out with all power. It can also represent a period of judgment. You notice my third book explained about the number seven and eight and also the love letter of the 12 tribes defined. Seven which is perfection and number eight new beginnings or new world or creation. So before new world or age or creation takes place, judgment comes first.

70 elders were appointed by Moses (Numbers 11:16-24) And Moses went out and told the people the words of the LORD, and gathered the seventy men of the elders of the people and set them round about the tabernacle.25 And the LORD came down in a cloud and spoke unto him, and took of the Spirit that was upon him and gave it unto the seventy elders; and it came to pass that, when the Spirit rested upon them, they prophesied, and did not cease.. After reading the covenant God gave him to read to the people, Moses took 70 elders, along with Aaron and his sons, up Mount Sinai to have a special meal with God himself (Exodus 24:9 - 11)! 9 Then went up Moses and Aaron, Nadab and Abihu, and seventy of the elders of Israel; 10 and they saw the God of Israel. And there was under His feet as it were a paved work of a sapphire stone, and as it were the body of heaven in his clearness.11 And upon the nobles of the children of Israel He laid not His hand. Also they saw God, and ate and drank.

You notice they meet with Yeshua and had communion with the Son of the living God. Paved work in Hebrew means a deed or an act taking place, sapphire stone in

Hebrew mean-with other jewels as ornaments of prince. Luke 10:1 After these things the Lord appointed seventy others also, and sent them two by two ahead of Him into every city and place whither He Himself would come. 17 And the seventy returned again with joy, saying, "Lord, even the devils are subject unto us through Thy name."

You notice they went in the Power of his Name Yeshua not Jesus Christ people, also they went with his Authority. This also resembles the 70 parables given by Yeshua the 4Gospels (Good news), the book of Matthew Salt of the earth (5:13)2.Light of the world (5:14)3.Birds of the air are fed by God (6:25- 26)4.Consider the Lilies and amazing flowers God has created (6:28-30)5.They will be known by their fruits (7:16-23)6.House built on a rock (7:24-27)7.The good physician (9:12-13)8.Friends of the Bridegroom (9:15-17)9.New cloth on old (9:16)10.New wine in old bottles (9:17)11.Children in the marketplace (11:16-17)12.Wisdom justified by children (11:18-19)13.Kingdom divided against itself (12:25-29)14.The unclean spirit that wanders and returns home (12:43-45)15.The Sower (13:3-23)16.Shine your light before the world (5:15-16)17.The Mustard seed (13:31- 32)18. Kingdom of God like leaven (13:33)19.Treasure hidden in a field (13:44)20.The costly pearl (13:45-46)21.Kingdom of God like a net (13:47-50)22.Scribe is like man who brings out old, new things (13:52)23.The Blind religious leaders of the blind (15:14-20)24.Become as little children (18:3-6)25.Offensive hands and eyes spiritually speaking (18:7-9)26.The lost sheep (18:12- 14)27.The unforgiving servant (18:23-35)28.The workers in the vineyard (20:1-6)29.One faithful and one rebellious son (21:28-32)30.The evil servants in God's vineyard (21:33-46)31.The wedding feast (22:1-14)32. Vultures and the carcasses (24:28) 33. Fig tree seasons like seasons of prophecy (24:32-35)34.The watchful servants (24:42-51)35.The Ten Virgins (25:1-13)36.The talents (25:14-30)37.The Sheep and the Goats (25:31-46)

The book of Mark, The growing seed (4:26-29)

The book of Luke The book of Luke1. Creditor owed by two people (7:40-47)2.Good Samaritan (10:30-37)3.A friend needs food at midnight (11:5-8)4.Ask and it shall be given (11:9-10)5.The Giver of good gifts (11:11-13)6.The rich fool (12:16-22)7.Life is more than food and the body more than clothes (12:22-24)8.Barren fig tree (13:6-9)9.Narrow gate of salvation (13:24)10.Master refuses to open door of those who knock (13:25-30)11.Be humble (14:8-14)12.Cost of discipleship (14:26-33)13.The lost coin (15:8-10)14.Prodigal son (15:11- 32)15.Friends of mammon (16:1-9)16.Lazarus and the Rich man (16:19-31)17.Mustard seed faith (17:6)18.Unprofitable servant (17:7-10)19.The widow and the Judge (18:2-8)20.The Pharisee and the Tax Collector (18:10-14)21.Nobleman pays his ten servants (19:12-27)

The book of John The book of John1.The wind is like Holy Spirit (3:8)2.Fields are white for harvest (4:35-38)3.The Son follow the Father (5:19-20)4.Servant of sin freed by repentance and forgiveness through Jesus (8:35)5.The Good Shepherd (John 10:1-18)6.Make the most of your 12 waking hours of daylight (11:9-10)7.Wheat must die to live (12:23-25)8.Walking in the light (12:35-36)9.A place prepared (14:2-4)10.Christ is the True Vine (15:1-8)11.Weeping and rejoicing (16:20-22).So you have 38+21+11=70.

Also you see in Ezekiel 8:11 And there stood before them seventy men of the ancients of the house of Israel, and in the midst of them stood Jaazaniah the son of Shaphan (unclean animal); living in rocks, *coney* a small grouper (fish) found on the coasts of the tropical western Atlantic, with variable coloration. (Now you know where the fish symbol came from paganism) with every man his censer in his hand; and a thick cloud of incense went up.12 Then said He unto me, "Son of man, hast thou seen what the elders of the house of Israel do in the dark, every man in the chambers of his images? For they say, 'The LORD seethe us not. The LORD hath forsaken the earth.'" Everything God does Satan and his wickedness camouflages it to make it look like worship and accreditation unto Yahweh. 14 Then He brought me to the door of the gate of the Lord's house which was toward the north; and behold, there sat women weeping for Tammuz. Intercessors weeping and worshiping to the God of Vegetation cycle, the Babylonian god of the vegetation cycle, believed to die annually, descend to the netherworld, and then rise again, corresponding to the changing of the seasons; Tammuz originated as a Sumerian god Dumu-zid or Dumuzi and in Babylonia a month was named in honor of Tammuz.

16 And He brought me into the inner court of the Lord's house, and behold, at the door of the temple of the LORD, between the porch and the altar, were about five and twenty men with their backs toward the temple of the LORD and their faces toward the east; and they worshiped the sun toward the east. Now you notice beasts, fish and sun gods, these are Greek worship, Egyptian worship, pagan worship and Persian Gods. You notice what does this resemble, this is happening in the inner court today by

the church. As the worshipers off Bacchus waved their Thyrsus, The Roman god of wine and intoxication, equated with the Greek Dionysus. Thee *thyrsus*, associated with Dionysus (or Bacchus) and his followers, the Satyrs and Maenads, is a symbol of prosperity, fertility, hedonism, and pleasure/enjoyment in general. Hedonism (Prudential Hedonism holds that all and only pleasure intrinsically makes people's lives go better *for them* and all and only pain intrinsically makes their lives go worse *for them)*. So Yahweh is stating this demon god spirit is activated so strong all over the world they value pleasure above all.

So when you hear on National televised Church programs about Prosperity pleasure, sow your seed of certain amount of Money on your Credit card, and discern what sort of Demon God is speaking. The lusts of the flesh. This spirit has been strongly impregnated within the Spirit of Man. The 70 elders and intercessors represents the Leaders in the televised world and also the Church age here and now. So when you see someone acting in the Gifts of the Spirit and then say things like Money cometh to me now ,that's a Demon God speaking, mixture of the polluting of the anointing within them. As the worshipers of Bacchus waved their Thyrsus They stalk wreathed with ivy. Wreathed means to be in twined with ivy (Poison). Now you notice the verse said about five and twenty men turning their backs on God. Well we all know the church has turned their backs against the fivefold ministry, 20 means perfect waiting or expectancy, the opposite of waiting is instant gratification. Meaning in the Presence of Yahweh ministry today acts without the timing of his spirit, we need to move now, and there's no Spiritual timing going on.

Matthew 17:9 And as they came down from the mountain, Jesus charged them, saying, "Tell the vision to no man until the Son of Man be risen again from the dead."10 And His disciples asked Him, saying, "Why then say the scribes that Elijah must first come?"11 And Jesus answered and said unto them, "Elijah truly shall first come and restore all things.12 But I say unto you that Elijah is come already, and they knew him not, but have done unto him whatsoever they pleased. Likewise shall also the Son of Man suffer by them." 13 Then the disciples understood that He spoke unto them of John the Baptist. Daddy Yahweh is speaking of the Elijah ministries that will restore us back into the Garden of Eden before the Fall of man!

Isaiah 6:10 Make the heart of this people fat (Circumcision to cut heart), and make their ears heavy, and shut their eye (Closed their hearts to hear the revelations); lest they see with their eyes, and hear with their ears, and understand with their heart, and convert and be healed (It also means to be received and returned into their glorified body."11 Then said I, "Lord, how long?" And He answered, "Until the cities be wasted without inhabitant, and the houses without man, and the land be utterly desolate(save me from this dead religion),12 and the LORD have removed men far away, and there be a great forsaking in the midst of the land.13 "But yet in it shall be a tenth, and it shall return and shall be eaten, as a teil tree and as an oak whose substance is in them when they cast their leaves: so the holy seed shall be the substance thereof." The Father is saying I still have an offering which is my remnant, through this move and this tenth, Elijah ministries I am bringing the restoration of all things.

But now Christ is risen from the dead, and has become **the first fruits of those who have fallen asleep**. For since by man came death, by Man also came the resurrection of the dead. For as in Adam all die, even so in Christ all shall be made alive. But **each one in his own order: Christ the first fruits**, afterward those who are Christ's at His coming (1 Corinthians 15:20-23). Now you notice this has nothing to do with Tithe or the First fruits of money or your increase to pay a Tithe at all. Now who were the First Jews the 12 apostles, how many were in the upper room on the day of Pentecost 120 so what 12 Divided by 120 equals=10. This is symbolic of the remnant of Yahweh redemption to restore all things.

In my third book I spoke of three fruits missing, from the scriptures of the bible, we only see 9fruits recorded, love-joy-peace-long suffering-kindness-goodness-faithfulness-gentleness-self control. The bible speaks of Righteousness (Holiness living sanctified, Truth which is his word, Praise always worshiping him). You also notice the Catholics have 12fruits the three recorded are Generosity, Charity and Chastity. You notice from my third book Satan had only 9stones, meaning even the scriptures of the fruits were not interpreted in the regular nine there should have been possibly 12. You notice did not Satan, was he not the Number one Worshiper in heaven.

CHAPTER 4

Let's move on Saints Luke 12:36 and ye yourselves like unto men that wait for their lord when he will return from the wedding, that when he cometh and knocketh, they may open unto him immediately (being prepared spiritually and circumcised in your heart).37 Blessed are those servants whom the lord, when he cometh, shall find watching (Open ears to hear the revelations of his Spirit). Verily I say unto you, that he shall gird himself and make them to sit down to eat (To eat of this Manna and drink new wine), and will come forth and serve them.38 And if he shall come in the second watch, or come in the third watch and find them so, blessed are those servants.39 And this know, that if the master of the house had known what hour the thief would come, he would have watched and not have suffered his house to be broken into. What thief or spirit is breaking into your mind, body, soul, spirit and heart?

40 Be ye therefore ready also, for the Son of Man cometh at an hour when ye think not."41 Then Peter said unto Him, "Lord, speakest Thou this parable unto us, or even to all?"42 And the Lord said, "Who then is that faithful and wise steward, whom his lord shall make ruler over his household, to give them their portion of meat in due season? Your portion of mysteries and secrets of revelation and understanding in your due time or season is being prepared now eat of it.

46 the lord of that servant will come in a day when he looketh not for him, and at an hour when he is not aware, and will cut him asunder and will appoint him his portion

with the unbelievers. You will receive your portion in how he wants to distribute his will upon you or in you. 47 And that servant, who knew his lord's will and prepared not himself, neither did according to his will, shall be beaten with many stripes. When the revelation is being poured forth the stripes resembles the seals of his markings to be whipped into you for his good pleasure. 48 But he that knew not and committed things worthy of stripes, shall be beaten with few stripes. For unto whomsoever much is given, of him shall much be required; and to whom men have committed much, of him they will ask the more.

Now let me give you the understanding of increase and wealth, when it pertains to money, prosperity and success saints. Talent in Hebrew means round coin usually silver or gold, also it means, a round loaf of bread. It also means Morsel, when bread is made theirs no nutrients in the crust outside only when you break the bread that is considered the morsel that was hidden within the bread. Morsel is the hidden word and revelation that comes out of the bread. There is life in the morsel, just like a kernel, is there nutrients in the shell or life in the seed. Yahweh's economy is hidden within the Morsel, his word of the Holy Spirit of revelation and understanding. That is his financial wealth increase, so get as much parables and mysteries and secrets and eat because it never ends or stops.

Here is the Revelation in Psalms 1: Blessed is the man that walketh not in the counsel of the ungodly, nor standeth in the way of sinners, nor sitteth in the seat of the scornful; 2 but his delight is in the law of the LORD, and on His law doth he meditate day and night. Law is his teachings of his spirit, the manna, His revelations of understanding. 3 And he shall be like a tree planted by the rivers of water that bringeth forth his fruit in his season; his leaf also shall not wither, and whatsoever he doeth shall prosper. It specifically states meditate on his word day and night and everything he does shall prosper.

Saints here is another comparison to what I speak of, Revelation 16:21 And there fell upon men a great hail (Hard rain-Hard word of revelation very difficult to digest) out of heaven, every hailstone (Deep heavy revelation-bread manna) about the weight of a talent (Morsel, hidden manna of his word, mystery of the kingdom). And men blasphemed God because of the plague (The true teachings spread) of the hail, for the plague thereof was exceeding great. The mysteries of the kingdom of revelation was to heavy and great they Blasphemed Yahweh for it. Now you notice it stated Hailstone, while we human beings are made of water 78%, then stone means hardness of heart or ignorance or we have prehistoric seeds within us. Meaning how hard would it be to break through and crack open to get to the soil within you. Basically it could also mean all of us are hardheaded stubborn mules.

Satan is fighting over two things and others but two specific, he does not want you to worship or dance before him constantly and receive his word of revelation and understanding. Matthew 4:3 And when the tempter came to Him, he said, "If Thou be the Son of God, command that these stones be made bread."4 But He answered and said, "It is written: 'Man shall not live by bread alone, but by every word that proceedeth out of the mouth of God.'" Turn the manna bread into simple regular doctrine, meaning twist this word and pour mixture into it, because Satan wanted a different recipe for it. Amos 3:7 Surely the

Lord GOD will do nothing, unless He revealeth His secret unto His servants the prophets.

Ephesians 2:20 Ye are built upon the foundation of the apostles and prophets, Jesus Christ Himself being the chief cornerstone. Is there any Apostles and Prophets in your temple or church building, does is say that the pastor is in control of the flock, does it say bishop, evangelists, teacher etc. So only Apostles and Prophets are in charge in the church or service building and only secrets mysteries and revelations come to His Apostles and Prophets yes even his intercessors!.

Saint there is more Interest in Hebrew Neshek-(Interest on a loan, a primitive root to bite as with a sting, as a serpent, figuratively to bite or oppress on a loan. Debt in Hebrew means deception, there is a pictograph representing continuance, also another pictograph from the Hebrew word (Shin), resembles teeth, representing pressure. It means continual pressing, in English it means to gnash. This means when you're in debt you're chewing on nothing, no meat or revelation or understanding of his word. Plus when you here this voice sow your seed, or give an offering with your credit card, which causes debt and interest, you just fell into witchcraft. Debt also means the removal of a debt forgetting or forgiving.

Which also means when you ask for forgiveness and repenting for the removal of our transgressions, iniquities, sins and the deception to be removed out of us.

Luke 13:28"In that place there will be weeping and gnashing of teeth when you see Abraham and Isaac and Jacob and all the prophets in the kingdom of God, but yourselves being thrown out. Abraham means father of multitude or abundance, Isaac means he laughs Psalms 2: He that sitteth in the heavens shall laugh: the Lord shall have them in derision (to mock or ridicule).Jacob in Hebrew means (Yahweh Protects), Mark 9:18 and whenever it seizes him, it slams him to the ground and he foams at the mouth, and grinds his teeth and stiffens out. I told your disciples to cast it out, and they could not do it." When you get bitten by a snake which is interest, and you're in debt which means you gnash your teeth, it destroys your immune system spiritually and physically. When you chew on false doctrine, or just the simple doctrine of the word without no Holy Spirit in it.

There is more to this revelation, Mark 9:18 And wheresoever he taketh him, he teareth him; and he foameth and gnasheth his teeth and pineth away. And I spoke to thy disciples that they should cast him out, and they could not." Foameth in Hebrew means to crack or break or convulse with spasms. Your emotions and feelings are shattered with no joy, the bible says the joy of the lord is our strength. Now watch this next the verse says 22 And oftentimes it hath cast him into the fire and into the waters to destroy him; but if thou canst do anything, have compassion on us and help us." You notice fire in Hebrew means for refining or wickedness Isaiah 9:18 For wickedness burneth as the fire; it shall devour the briers and thorns, and shall kindle in the thickets of the forest, and they shall mount up like the lifting up of smoke.19 Through the wrath of the LORD of hosts is the land darkened, and the people shall be as the fuel of the fire; no man shall spare his brother.

49

Furthermore it states water to destroy it, Luke 8:43 And a woman (Church) having an issue of blood for twelve years (12 tribes of Israel Remnant) who had spent all her living upon physicians but could not be healed by any, 44 came behind Him and touched the border of His garment; and immediately her issue of blood was stanched.46 And Jesus said, "Somebody hath touched Me, for I perceive that virtue is gone out of Me." Virtue is a form of water also, the Holy Spirit, the spirit of living waters. 2 Corinthians 11:14And no marvel; for Satan himself is transformed into an angel of light. OK Saints you're asking where is this analogy coming from well, it states further Mark 9:25 When Jesus saw that the people came running together, He rebuked the foul spirit, saying unto him, "Thou dumb and deaf spirit, I charge thee, come out of him and enter no more into him." Dumb means ignorant of satans devices, also could mean stubborn or disobedient, also deaf means what empty, hardheaded no room for counsel. Deaf in Hebrew means deaf adder(Any of several groups of venomous snakes), Psalms 58;5 So that it does not hear the voice of charmers, Or a skillful caster of spells, so that it cannot hear the voice of a snake charmer or of anyone trained to cast spells.

Now how come they could not cast this spirit out of him a certain kind of spirit, well here is one Revelation Mark 9:2 And after six days Jesus took with Him Peter and James and John, and led them up onto a high mountain apart by themselves; and He was transfigured before them. Verse 18 And I spoke to thy disciples that they should cast him out, and they could not." 28 And when He had come into the house, His disciples asked Him privately, "Why could not we cast him out?"29 And He said unto them, "This kind can come forth by nothing but by prayer and fasting."

Prayer is a form of repenting from old ways, also fasting means in Hebrew means weakened physically to have leanness of the soul, also means he was troubled in his mind. Psalms 109:24 My knees give way from fasting, and my skin is lean, deprived of oil(Lack of understanding in the mind).Matthew 16:23 But he turned and said unto Peter, Remove thyself from before me, Satan; thou art an offense unto me, for thou dost not understand that which is of God, but that which is of men.

The Disciples had the same deaf and dumb spirit, lack of understanding, the apostles did not receive the fullness of the Shekinah glory until the Book of Acts, the upper room experience when the fire came down and burned out all the Carnality out of their minds. Luke 9:28 Now about eight days after these teachings, Jesus took with Him Peter and John and James and went up on the mountain to pray. 46 But a controversy arose among them as to which of them might be the greatest [surpassing the others in excellence, worth, and authority]. Luke 9:58 And Jesus said unto him, Foxes have holes, and birds of the air *have* nests; but the Son of man hath not where to lay *his* head. In the bible is states to put on the mind of Christ. 1 Corinthians 2:16 For who hath known the mind of the Lord, that he may instruct him?

But we have the mind of Christ. Yeshua specifically states I have no one to put my head upon them, which a resemblance to put my understanding within them or to have the mind of the Yeshua.

Mark 9:32 But they did not comprehend what He was saying, and they were afraid to ask Him [what this statement meant]. 34 But they kept still, for on the road

51

they had discussed *and* disputed with one another as to who was the greatest. James and John fighting amongst one another arguing who is the greatest in the kingdom. 35 And He sat down and called the Twelve [apostles], and He said to them, If anyone desires to be first, he must be last of all, and servant of all.

Now let's move on saints 1 Corinthians 15:5 54 So when this corruptible shall have put on in corruption, and this mortal shall have put on immortality, then shall be brought to pass the saying that is written: "Death is swallowed up in victory."55 "O death, where is thy sting? O grave, where is thy victory?" Now you notice Interest in Hebrew means to have a sting also correct, usury or bite by a serpent, the enemy can put you in hell because of your ignorance.56 The sting of death is sin, and the strength of sin is the law. Meaning ignorance of his word is death and strength, revelation and understanding of his word is life. Sting in Greek means Kentron a sharp point also, sting (1. a sting, as that of bees (4 Macc. 14:19), scorpions, locusts.

Joel 1:6 A vast army of locusts[b] has invaded my land, a terrible army too numerous to count. Its teeth are like lions' teeth, its fangs like those of a lioness.7 It has destroyed my grapevines and ruined my fig trees, stripping their bark and destroying it, leaving the branches white and bare.8 Weep like a bride dressed in black, mourning the death of her husband.9 For there is no grain or wine to offer at the Temple of the Lord. So the priests are in mourning. The ministers of the LORD are weeping.10 The fields are ruined, the land is stripped bare. The grain is destroyed, the grapes have shriveled, and the olive oil is gone.11 Despair, all you farmers! Wail, all you vine growers! Weep, because the wheat and barley—all the crops of the field—are ruined.12 The grapevines have dried up, and the fig trees have withered. The pomegranate trees, palm trees, and apple trees—all the fruit trees—have dried up. And the people's joy has dried up with them.

Now it states grapevine in Hebrew means, a vine bearing poisonous gourds, fig trees-to mature they came to ruin, stripping there bark in Hebrew and Greek means inner man-Isaiah 56:10 Israel's watchmen are blind, they all lack knowledge; they are all mute dogs, they cannot bark; they lie around and dream, they love to sleep. Leaving the branches us we are the branches, leaving us white in Hebrew (Laban) means of diseased skin or flesh on body (Leviticus 13:4 "If the light spot in the skin of his body is white but the appearance of the skin rash isn't deeper than the skin of his body and its hair has not become white, then the priest is to isolate the one who is infected for seven days. Bare in Hebrew Arah- to be naked or empty. Further it states there is no grain or wine to bring to Yeshua for Daddy to taste it and get an approval on it, grain which is food (Revelation or hidden manna-Wine Understanding or Shekinah glory anointing) also can be no communion between us with Yeshua! The field-their hearts and the ministry, land which is soil and us bare unclothed with no robes of righteousness. The grain is destroyed- the revelation and secrets and hidden manna has stopped, the grapes bear no fruit, oil is gone-no presence of the Eyeh Asher Eyeh with the Anointing of the Holy Spirit.

The pomegranate trees resembles 613 seeds or laws of the bible, the truth, palm in Hebrew trees- Umbels are a characteristic of plants such as carrot, parsley and dill, meaning fruits or inner man, apple tree in Greek and Hebrew tappuwach (Proverbs 25:110 Timely advice is lovely, like golden apples in a silver basket.

Joel1:13 Dress yourselves in burlap and weep, you priests! Wail, you who serve before the altar! Come, spend the night in burlap, you ministers of my God. For there is no grain or wine to offer at the Temple of your God.14 Announce a time of fasting; call the people together for a solemn meeting. Bring the leaders and all the people of the land into the Temple of the LORD your God, and cry out to him there.15 the day of the LORD is near, the day when destruction comes from the Almighty. How terrible that day will be. 16 Our food disappears before our very eyes. No joyful celebrations are held in the house of our God.17 The seeds die in the parched ground, and the grain crops fail. The barns (The ministry services) stand empty, and granaries (The people-manna) are abandoned.18 How the animals moan with hunger! The herds of cattle wander about confused, because they have no pasture. The flocks of sheep and goats bleat in misery.19 LORD, help us! The fire has consumed the wilderness pastures, and flames have burned up all the trees.20 Even the wild animals cry out to you because the streams have dried up, and fire has consumed the wilderness pastures.

Saints listen to this, Revelation 9:1 Then the fifth angel sounded: And I saw a star (Churches) fallen from heaven to the earth. To him was given the key to the bottomless pit (Means no secrets or revelation). 2 And he opened the bottomless pit, and smoke arose out of the pit like the smoke of a great furnace. So the sun and the air were darkened because of the smoke of the pit (The Army that was running). 3 Then out of the smoke locusts came upon the earth. And to them was given power, as the scorpions of the earth have power. 4 They were commanded not to harm the grass of the earth, or any green thing, or any tree, but only those men who do not have the seal of God on their foreheads. 5 And they were not given *authority* to kill them, but to torment them *for* five months. Their torment *was* like the torment of a scorpion when it strikes a man. 6 In those days men will seek death and will not find it; they will desire to die, and death will flee from them. In Greek and Hebrew the locusts are religion, they a have sting a bite, sting of a scorpion, stings with ignorance and deception causing interest of debt. They have the power to sting you those who are in the religion but not those who have the seal Mark of Eyeh Asher Eyeh of Revelation and understanding and teaching of the Holy Priest, not the Mark of the Beastly Mentality of Carnality of the world system 666.

Finally the Spirit of Yah and his army has two side. In the bible He states I am the God of Heaven and Earth I create Evil and good. Which army are you part of, In the Bible God even states I trap man in his own wisdom, 1 Corinthians 3:19 For the wisdom of this world is foolishness to God. As the Scriptures say, "He traps the wise in the snare of their own cleverness." Revelation 9: 7The locusts looked like horses prepared for battle. On their heads they wore something like crowns of gold, and their faces resembled human faces. 8Their hair was like women's hair, and their teeth were like lions' teeth. 9They had breastplates like breastplates of iron, and the sound of their wings was like the thundering of many horses and chariots rushing into battle. 10They had tails with stingers, like scorpions, and in their tails they had power to torment people for five months. 11They had as king over them the angel of the

Abyss, whose name in Hebrew is Abaddon and in Greek is Apollyon (that is, Destroyer).

You notice they had crown of gold on their heads and human faces this is Also Gods Army that was deceived by their own selves or the false doctrine and spirits of Satan. You notice also verse 10 they had power to torment people for five months, resembles apostolic church hurting or destroying their own kind also God's grace upon mankind. They were deceived by false spirit of Abaddon-Apollyon the Destroyer.

12The first woe is past; two other woes are yet to come. The Second woe is the Redemption of mankind and 7year revival and Inheritance of all what we been waiting for. Also the third woe is becoming immortal one with our father. Woe also means a transition or shift of great grandeur of bad and good. Revelation 21: And I heard a great voice out of heaven saying, Behold, the tabernacle of God *is* with men, and he will dwell with them, and they shall be his people, and God himself shall be with them, *and be* their God.

13The sixth angel sounded his trumpet, and I heard a voice coming from the four horns of the golden altar that is before God. **14**It said to the sixth angel who had the trumpet, "Release the four angels who are bound at the great river Euphrates." **15**And the four angels who had been kept ready for this very hour and day and month and year were released to kill a third of mankind. **16**The number of the mounted troops was twice ten thousand times ten thousand. I heard their number.

17The horses and riders I saw in my vision looked like this: Their breastplates were fiery red, dark blue, and yellow as sulfur. The heads of the horses resembled the heads of lions, and out of their mouths came fire, smoke and sulfur. **18**A third of mankind was killed by the three plagues of fire, smoke and sulfur that came out of their mouths. **19**The power of the horses was in their mouths and in their tails; for their tails were like snakes, having heads with which they inflict injury.

Dark blue water river of God, cleansing life giving flow of the Holy Spirit, the Word ruler ship, unlimited potential, priesthood(Esther 8:15) Red blood of Jesus, atonement, grace. Yellow joy, revelation. Saints verse 17 mouths came fire Prophecy, smoke the dew of Heaven his Presence and sulfur brimstone also means to Purify the Heart!. Also they had tails like snakes, be sharp as a serpent soft as a dove, having heads to inflict injury, Hebrews 4:12 for the word of God is alive and active. Sharper than any double-edged sword, it penetrates even to dividing soul and spirit, joints and marrow; it judges the thoughts and attitudes of the heart.

20The rest of mankind who were not killed by these plagues still did not repent of the work of their hands; they did not stop worshiping demons, and idols of gold, silver, bronze, stone and wood—idols that cannot see or hear or walk. **21**Nor did they repent of their murders, their magic arts, their sexual immorality or their thefts.

1 John 2:15 Do not love the world (1) or the things that belong to[c] the world (2). If anyone loves the world (3), love for the Father is not in him. 16 For everything that belongs to[d] the world (4)—the lust of the flesh, the lust of the eyes, and the pride in one's lifestyle—is not from

the Father, but is from the world (5). 17 And the world (6) with its lust is passing away, but the one who does God's will remains forever.

Saints most of you cannot stay away from religious systems, cause you continue to get bite over and over listening to the wrong teaching, the church or services you attend, plus the books you read, and the other locusts you hang around with because of their great fame and titles they carry. We continue to untwist you and burn it out but you jump from here to there.

Revelation 9:7 The shape of the locusts was like horses prepared for battle. On their heads were crowns of something like gold, and their faces *were* like the faces of men. 8 They had hair like women's hair, and their teeth were like lions' *teeth.* 9 And they had breastplates like breastplates of iron, and the sound of their wings *was* like the sound of chariots with many horses running into battle. 10 They had tails like scorpions, and there were stings in their tails. Their power *was* to hurt men five months. 11 And they had as king over them the angel of the bottomless pit, whose name in Hebrew *is* Abaddon, but in Greek he has the name Apollyon. The Father is speaking about his army with no revelation or secrets, no intimacy, the powerless church, no communion. Where are all the locusts they are mostly all in the dead churches in the bottomless pit, the spirit of Abaddon and Appolyn the majority of the church.

The Apostles and Prophets are there to pay off your interests and debts, by the secrets and economic kingdom of Eyeh Asher Eyeh of his word, through secrets, mysteries and revelations of true doctrine. Revelation 1:20 As to the hidden meaning (the mystery) of the seven stars which you saw on My right hand and the seven lamp stands of gold: the seven stars are the seven angels (messengers) of the seven assemblies (churches) and the seven lamp stands are the seven churches.

Here is an illustration of witchcraft be a good Stewart with your money, hello twist and sting. Sow your seed and put your seed in the offering basket, sting a bite. So when you're putting your money in that teaching your putting your money in the Kingdom of Abbadon, Appolyon and Darkness the bottomless pit. You are investing in the enemy's War, against the Apostolic and Eyeh Asher Eyeh true army, you are funding their mascaraed. You notice in the bible it states they sold houses land etc. and presented at the feet of the Apostles, not the bishop, reverend, pastor, evangelist, teacher etc.

Matthew 18:15 "If your brother sins against you, [h] go and rebuke him in private. [I] If he listens to you, you have won your brother. 16 But if he won't listen, take one or two more with ȳou, so that by the testimony[j] of two or three witnesses every fact may be established.[k] 17 If he pays no attention to them, tell the church.[l] But if he doesn't pay attention even to the church, let him be like an unbeliever[m] and a tax collector to you. You are to correct your brother when he does not understand the word by the spirit. If he does not pay attention treat him like an unbeliever who is not saved. So technically only those who are allowing Yeshua to circumcise their hearts are truly those who are saved.

Let me give you another Mystery Matthew 18:21 Then Peter came to Him and said, "Lord, how many times could my brother sin against me and I forgive him? As many as seven times?"22 "I tell you, not as many as seven," Jesus said to him, "but 70 times seven. This mystery is recorded in the book of Daniel.

Daniel Declares the End, or new life, Daniel 9:20 While I was speaking, praying, confessing my sin and the sin of my people Israel, and presenting my petition before Yahweh my God concerning the holy mountain of my God— 21 while I was praying, Gabriel, the man I had seen in the first vision, came to me in my extreme weariness, about the time of the evening offering. 22 He gave me this explanation: "Daniel, I've come now to give you understanding. 23 At the beginning of your petitions an answer went out, and I have come to give it, for you are treasured by God. So consider the message and understand the vision:24 Seventy weeks[d] are decreed about your people and your holy city—to bring the rebellion to an end, to put a stop to sin, to wipe away iniquity, to bring in everlasting righteousness, to seal up vision and prophecy, and to anoint the most holy place. This means to come out of the Babylonian Mentality, 7oyears. When did Israel become a Nation? In 1948, add 70 years to that, what do you get 2018 My beloved Saints!

OK Saints listen to this Daniel 9:Know and understand this: From the issuing of the decree to restore and rebuild Jerusalem until Messiah the Prince[e](Universal Gods One with him)will be seven weeks and 62 weeks.[f]It will be rebuilt with a plaza and a moat, but in difficult times.26 After those 62 weeks[g]the Messiah will be cut off and will have nothing(Has not the messiah right now been cut off, the Jewish orthodox wants to sacrifice animals in the new temple already).The people of the coming prince (False prince) will destroy the city and the sanctuary. The[h] end will come with a flood(The new Hundred dollar bill has blue water bells and you fold it a certain way has a pictograph of a nuclear missile being launched and cast into the water creating a flood or tsunami and waves over running city and buildings),and until the end there will be[l] war; desolation's are decreed(Is not there war with Russia and America, Syria and Jerusalem.27 He will make a firm covenant[j]with many for one week,[k]but in the middle of the week he will put a stop to sacrifice and offering. And the abomination of desolation will be on a wing of the temple[l] [m]until the decreed destruction is poured out on the desolator."

We are in the 70 year tribulation right now, we will have five more red blood moons, which only occurred twice in history, when three red blood moons in one year which happened in 1948 when Israel became a nation and 1967 the six day war. The war was against Syria, Jordan and Egypt. Israel believed that it was only a matter of time before the three Arab states coordinated a massive attack on Israel.

After the 1956 Suez Crisis, the United Nations had established a presence in the Middle East, especially at sensitive border areas. The United Nations was only there with the agreement of the nations that acted as a host to it. By May 1967, the Egyptians had made it clear that the United Nations was no longer wanted in the Suez region. Gamal Nasser, leader of Egypt, ordered a concentration of Egyptian military forces in the sensitive Suez zone. This was a highly provocative act and the Israelis only viewed it one way — that Egypt was preparing to attack. The Egyptians had also enforced a naval blockade which closed off the Gulf of Aqaba to Israeli shipping.

Rather than wait to be attacked, the Israelis launched a hugely successful military campaign against its perceived enemies. The air forces of Egypt, Jordan, Syria and Iraq were all but destroyed on June 5th. By June 7th, many Egyptian tanks had been destroyed in the Sinai Desert and Israeli forces reached the Suez Canal. On the same day, the whole of the west bank of the Jordan River had been cleared of Jordanian forces. The Golan Heights were captured from Syria and Israeli forces moved 30 miles into Syria itself.

The war was a disaster for the Arab world and temporarily weakened the man who was seen as the leader of the Arabs – Gamal Abdul Nasser of Egypt. The war was a military disaster for the Arabs but it was also a massive blow to the Arabs morale. Here were four of the strongest Arab nations systematically defeated by just one nation.

Matthew 18:23 For this reason, the kingdom of heaven can be compared to a king who wanted to settle accounts with his slaves. 24 When he began to settle accounts, one who owed 10,000 talents[s] was brought before him. 25 Since he had no way to pay it back, his master commanded that he, his wife, his children, and everything he had be sold to pay the debt.26 "At this, the slave fell face down before him and said, 'Be patient with me, and I will pay you everything!' 27 Then the master of that slave had compassion, released him, and forgave him the loan. Saints remember the parable of the talents, Matthew 25:14-30, the talents represent one who has received understanding and much wisdom. Some had five, two and the one who had only one and buried it. The one who had only one, did not want to multiply his understanding and correction or receive more revelation and increase in his spirit man.

Then Yeshua said give it to the one who had ten talents, because when you receive or eat from the one that has much revelation and understanding you shall receive much abundance.

So Saints watch this the Symbolic meaning of Ten Thousand, Daniel 7:9 I kept looking until thrones were placed [for the assessors with the Judge], and the Ancient of Days [God, the eternal Father] took His seat, Whose garment was white as snow and the hair of His head like pure wool. His throne was like the fiery flame; its wheels were burning fire.

A stream of fire came forth from before Him; a thousand thousands ministered to Him and ten thousand times ten thousand rose up *and* stood before Him; the Judge was seated [the court was in session] and the books were opened. Jude 1:4 And Enoch also, the seventh from Adam, prophesied of these, saying, "Behold, the Lord cometh with ten thousand of His saints. This is a symbolic remnant, according to the Rabbis they state these are the ones who receive the mark of Yahweh on their foreheads.

Revelation 5:11 Then I looked, and I heard the voice of many angels around the throne, the living creatures, and the elders; and the number of them was ten thousand times ten thousand, and thousands of thousands, 12 saying with a loud voice. This symbolic meaning is the remnant, the ten thousands, also the thousands of thousand is the 12tribes of Israel the same remnant. The Four living creatures are the eyes, all around the seraphim's and cherubim, Elijah ministries, the elders, the 24 elders reigning with Christ is symbolic same meaning, the 12tribes of Israel, 12 Foundations, which were the 12names of the Apostles. Which resembles complete Dominion and

Authority. This revelation is recorded also in my Third book, the unveiled secrets and mysteries of the Kingdom.

The ten thousands means those who understand the torah his truth and eats the mysteries and secrets of the kingdom coming from the true Apostles and Prophets. You notice sin Daniel 7:9 says thousand, which means 1,000, but then says thousands of thousands which is more than a thousand, which also means a double figure 44=44,000. Then it states Ten thousand times Ten Thousand which also means within the hundreds of thousands, which symbolically states in the Hundreds of Thousands. Revelation 7:7 After this I saw four angels standing at the four corners of the earth, holding back the four winds of the earth, that no wind might blow on earth or sea or against any tree. 2 Then I saw another angel ascending from the rising of the sun, with the seal of the living God, and he called with a loud voice to the four angels who had been given power to harm earth and sea, 3 saying, "Do not harm the earth or the sea or the trees, until we have sealed the servants[a] of our God on their foreheads." 4 And I heard the number of the sealed, 144,000, sealed from every tribe of the sons of Israel. Saints each tribe which were 12 had more than 12,000 Judea etc. etc.

CHAPTER 5

Now remember we spoke about a tenth which resembles only his remnant will remain, remember the 12 Apostles and there was 120 Jews in the upper room on day of Pentecost, normally there was 500, but the majority left, the tenth resembles small portion. This means 12 divided by 120 equals 10. Now let's considered some symbolic meanings, a thousand thousands, which means 000 and then six zeros 000,000's. It does state 10,000 times 10,000 which equals 100,000,000. While according to some studies there is approximately 7.125 billion people or more on this earth, a tenth of that would be 700,000,000 possibly only those who would receive the Mark of Yahweh on their foreheads I don't know just given out some symbolism's here. While according to the time prophetic meaning, time is a score=20 the thousand, times=40 , which thousands and then you notice it starts by saying Ten thousand x Ten thousand, while if you separate the thousand it only remains a 10,so 20+40+10=70. OK lets categorize it 100,000,000, a thousand 000 taken off and then thousands which is the next set of zeros which remaineth 100 divided by 10=10 a tenth.

Yes Saints symbolically I am referring to the Daniel symbolic meaning also, which was already described in my third book, Daniel 12:7 And I heard the man clothed in linen, who was above the waters of the river, when he held up his right and his left hand toward the heavens and swore by Him Who lives forever that it shall be for a time, times, and a half a time [or three and one-half years]; and when they have made an end of shattering *and* crushing the power of the holy people, all these things shall be finished. This revelation is in my third book, my first book The Seed of Resurrection, Second The Fruits of Favor and Increase, Third book called Apocalypse Encrypted. Saints I am comparing this symbolic symbol to this verse recorded in the bible, Daniel 12:7 times, times and half of time, also Daniel 7:9 it states thousand thousands and then Ten thousand times Ten thousand. Time = Thousand, Times=Thousands well what's the half of time resemble ½. Well the one resembles a Digit number is the ten, is the same Ten, The 2 resembles there are two of the same Digit number. Ten thousand times Ten thousand of the same Digit number 10. The Digit number 10,000 needs to be multiplied by the same Digit number it expresses. There is two Digit numbers which have the same comparison and equality, but remaineth the same as one, there is no separation. These have a similar comparison of scripture symbolically but have multiple revelations in them.

Tribulation already happened what Daniel speaks of **Dec. 1941** extermination camps operational <31/2years —> extermination camps liberated **May 1945"God's people will be helpless in his hands for three and a half years** "Daniel 7:25 *The Living Bible* Survivors would 'possess the kingdom' Israel (1948) Daniel 7:22,27. This is one Revelation.

Now in my third book I spoke of Immortality, the Tabernacle age, the Kingdom age, more revelation concerning this Revelation 5:8 Now when He had taken the scroll, the four living creatures and the twenty-four elders fell down before the Lamb, each having a harp, and golden bowls full of incense, which are the prayers of the saints. 9 And they sang a new song, saying: "You are worthy to take the scroll, And to open its seals; For You were slain, and have redeemed us to God by Your blood.

Out of every tribe and tongue and people and nation, 10 and have made us kings and priests to our God; and we shall reign on the earth."11 Then I looked, and I heard the voice of many angels around the throne, the living creatures, and the elders; and the number of them was ten thousand times ten thousand, and thousands of thousands, 12 saying with a loud voice: "Worthy is the Lamb who was slain To receive power and riches and wisdom, And strength and honor and glory and blessing!"13 And every creature which is in heaven and on the earth and under the earth and such as are in the sea, and all that are in them, I heard saying: "Blessing and honor and glory and *power Be* to Him who sits on the throne, And to the Lamb, forever and ever!" 14 Then the four living creatures said, "Amen!" And the twenty- four elders fell down and worshiped Him who lives forever and ever.

The four living creature are the seraphim's and cherubim, which had all eyes all around, remember we are the messengers and the Elijah ministries his remnant, the menorah which had 7 spirits of God. Also the menorah had almond buds on them representing in Hebrew they are eyes watching, Jeremiah   1:11 Moreover, the word of the Lord came to me, saying, Jeremiah, what do you see? And I said, I see a branch *or* shoot of an almond tree [the emblem of alertness and activity, blossoming in late winter].12 Then said the Lord to me, you have seen well, for I am alert *and* active, watching over My word to perform it. We become the eyes of Yahweh, the 24 elders Complete Dominion and Authority, each having a harp a minstrel of praise, worship, golden bowls of incense, prayer of the saints. In Hebrew prayer means to burn incense in worship. It states we shall become Kings and Priests here on earth and rule and reign. It also specifically states You will receive Power (Universal power), Riches beyond your unfathomable understanding, Wisdom beyond all recognition In the Heavens there are University of books limitless, Strength (Exactly Like a God in the natural, earthly form),Honor (Prince), Glory (Immortality) form of Yeshua exact likeness, Blessing (They shall Inherit all things).

Revelation 21:11 Clothed in God's glory [in all its splendor and radiance]. The luster of it resembled a rare *and* most precious jewel, like jasper, shining clear as crystal. Revelation 4:11 And He who was sitting was like a jasper stone and a sardius in appearance; and there was a rainbow around the throne, like an emerald in appearance. Jasper speaking of the (Prince Yeshua). We shall be clothed in Gods Glory, exact likeness, 1 Corinthians 15:49 And just as we have borne the image [of the man] of dust, so shall we *and so let us* also bear the image [of the Man] of heaven. 50 But I tell you this, brethren, flesh and blood cannot [become partakers of eternal salvation and] inherit *or* share in the kingdom of God; nor does the perishable (that which is decaying) inherit *or* share in the imperishable (the immortal).

51 Take notice! I tell you a mystery (a secret truth, an event decreed by the hidden purpose or counsel of God). We shall not all fall asleep [in death], but we shall all be changed (transformed) In a moment, in the twinkling of an eye, at the [sound of the] last trumpet call. For a trumpet will sound, and the dead [in Christ] will be raised

imperishable (free and immune from decay), and we shall be changed (transformed).53 For this perishable [part of us] must put on the imperishable [nature], and this mortal [part of us, this nature that is capable of dying] must put on immortality (freedom from death).54 And when this perishable puts on the imperishable and this that was capable of dying puts on freedom from death, then shall be fulfilled the Scripture that says, Death is swallowed up (utterly vanquished [h]forever) in *and* unto victory. Saints from one moment in time, the trumpet is the Prophets and Apostles speaking unto us the secrets and mysteries, the dead in Christ blind spiritually and physically, will put on imperishable never decay or die, we shall be transformed.

52 Furthermore Saints Romans 8:29 For those whom He foreknew [of whom He was [k]aware and [l]loved beforehand], He also destined from the beginning [foreordaining them] to be molded into the image of His Son [and share inwardly His likeness], that He might become the firstborn among many Brethren.30 And those whom He thus foreordained, He also called; and those whom He called, He also justified (acquitted, made righteous, putting them into right standing with Himself). And those whom He justified, He also glorified [raising them to a heavenly dignity and condition or state of being].

Once we have been molded into the image of his son, character and conduct, the inward likeness, raising us to a heavenly dignity beyond comprehension, conditions state of being Yeshua in exact superman) here on earth the Tabernacle, Kingdom age Eonian, 1,ooo year reign here on earth. Psalms 17: 14 From men by Your hand, O Lord, from men of *this* world [these poor moths of the night] whose portion in life is idle *and* vain. Their bellies are filled with

Your hidden treasure [what You have stored up]; their children are satiated, and they leave the rest [of their] wealth to their babes.

15 As for me, I will continue beholding Your face in righteousness (rightness, justice, and right standing with You); I shall be fully satisfied, when I awake [to find myself] beholding Your form [and having sweet communion with You]. Moths are idle vain carnal Christians who eat and chew on anything, Butterflies which are radiant and beautiful, before you transform into the Butterfly stage, there are four stages. The first stage is the egg, the sperm which Yahweh place in us permanently, 1 John 3:1 See what [an incredible] quality of love the Father has given (shown, bestowed on) us, that we should [be permitted to] be named *and* called *and* counted the children of God! And so we are! The reason that the world does not know (recognize, acknowledge) us is that it does not know (recognize, acknowledge) Him.

2 Beloved, we are [even here and] now God's children; it is not yet disclosed (made clear) what we shall be [hereafter], but we know that when He comes *and* is manifested, we shall [as God's children] resemble *and* be like Him, for we shall see Him just as He [really] is.3 And everyone who has this hope [resting] on Him cleanses (purifies) himself just as He is pure (chaste, undefiled, guiltless).

The father states they do not acknowledge him cause their mindsets of twisted teachings of doctrine and spirits, poisoned eggs, false impregnation etc. The second stage is caterpillar stage, you then begin to eat and you choose what to eat, you begin to grow and expand into immaturity of his word milk, or maturity meat and secrets and mysteries dying to self, laying down your self will, circumcise your heart. You notice the third stage, we are in the year 2014, the outer court 1day, 2nd day the inner court menorah the church age, 3day the Tabernacle Holy of Holies stage, Pupa (Chrysalis) Within the chrysalis the old body parts of the caterpillar are undergoing a remarkable transformation, called 'metamorphosis,' to become the beautiful parts that make up the butterfly that will emerge. Tissue, limbs and organs of a caterpillar have all been changed by the time the pupa is finished, and is now ready for the final stage of a butterfly's life cycle. The fourth stage is the Butterfly it transforms into. I'm just showing this analogy as symbolic meaning. The fourth stage is considered when Yeshua returns after the 1,000 year reign here on earth. The fourth stage is a comparison of the 3rd stage while you're a butterfly and come into this transformation process, your living out what you have eaten of the good things from the masters table preparing for the Wedding feast, being married to the Bride.

Also the second stage could be considered the first stage in a different form to be the walking stage of the transformation, your growing process, the form you have taken. So technically the first stage is the Caterpillar stage, the second is the transformation stage of what you're eating Pupa (Chrysalis), then third stage is the new Transformed body form, the butterfly. Now let me clarify about the 70weeks or 70 years, Israel became a nation in 1948, 70 from that times comes to what 2018. Today it is 2014 almost 2015, 10/06/2014, 3 ½ years of Abomination that causes Desolation, well the reverse side of this is the great falling away will be those who reject the Hard rain of Hailstones falling from the sky, the secrets and mysteries of the kingdom and they will Blasphemy God for it, of your heart is right and you're not offended it will not overtake you or consume you but transform you.

Deuteronomy 32:2 My message shall drop as the rain (Revelations), my speech shall distil as the dew, as the light rain upon the tender grass, and as the showers upon the herb. Deuteronomy Chap33:2 He said, The Lord came from Sinai and beamed upon us from Seir; He flashed forth from Mount Paran, from among ten thousands of holy ones, a flaming fire, a law, at His right hand.3 Yes, He loves [the tribes] His people; all those consecrated to Him are in Your hand. They followed in Your steps; they [accepted Your word and] received direction from You. Secrets of the mysteries which is the Cherubs with the Flaming Swords, those who have the Torah. Saints in the Movie Lucy gives an Symbolic meaning of Immortality, Then Morgan Freeman says to her this knowledge will only give making instability, do to its carnality and power and profit driven self, she stated only Ignorance brings instability and Destruction and Cause.

Saints lets continue Acts 9:7 And on the first day of the week, when we were assembled together to break bread [the Lord's Supper], Paul discoursed with them, intending to leave the next morning; and he kept on with his message until midnight.8 Now there were numerous lights in the upper room where we were assembled, And there was a young man named Eutychus sitting in the window. He was borne down with deep sleep as Paul kept on talking still longer, and [finally] completely overcome by sleep, he fell down from the third story and was picked up dead.10 But Paul went down and bent over him and embraced him, saying, Make no ado; his life is within him.11 When Paul had gone back upstairs and had broken bread and eaten [with them], and after he had talked confidentially *and* communed with them for a considerable time—until daybreak [in fact]—he departed.12Then the followers took the young man home alive they were happy.

You notice they Took Communion every time they went from house to house, there is power within this communion. Paul preached so long, he preached all night until the next day until midnight, meaning the ministering was so powerful and the revelation that were being brought out were amazing. Now saints when a religious demon tells you, well don't fall asleep during church, that is not what this teaching resembles. Saints first of all if you fall asleep in church its one or two things, one it's so boring with no Holy Spirit no life and no Gifts of the Holy Spirit moving at all its just Dead. Furthermore point two there is so much chaos in your life and in your household if the Holy spirit was really moving in that place, and the anointing was in the so called House of God, it would possibly put you to sleep, cause that's the only rest you're getting. There is another point of understanding here, Paul the Apostle moved in Demonstration and power, went to bend down and stated without further Ado, His life is within him, Paul brought him back to life.

The young man listened so long cause he was so enriched he stood that long listening by the mysteries and secrets being spoken. Then Paul the Apostle went back upstairs to break bread again taking communion and then preached Boldly again until Daybreak, the Apostle brought him back to life and still preached for another 5-6 hours possibly, then they took the young man home alive. Saints how come we don't take Communion like we should, Churches now a days, last only one hour, some Apostolic last three hours. Paul the Apostle ministers in Demonstration and Power of the Holy spirit, preaching so long and they went hungry and poor sometimes, raising the dead, healing the sick, paralyzed, blind eyes, those who can't walk, etc. Churches now a days have no Apostle or Prophet no demonstration or Power of the Holy Spirit and a lot of you still except this fact and give your money away to the wrong soil or aiding and funding these Circus acts all day few times a week. The Answer to all this is The Demonic General Demon of Ignorance is at large within the vessels of humans.

Isaiah 22:20 And in that day I will call My servant, Eliakim son of Hilkiah.21 And I will clothe him with your robe and will bind your girdle on him and will commit your authority to his hand; he shall be a father to the inhabitants of Jerusalem and to the house of Judah.22 And the key of the house of David I will lay upon his shoulder; he shall open and no one shall shut, he shall shut and no one shall open.23 And I will fasten him like a peg *or* nail in a firm place; and he will become a throne of honor *and* glory to his father's house.24 And they will hang on him the honor *and* the whole weight of [responsibility for] his father's house: the offspring and issue [of the family, high and low], every small vessel, from the cups even to all the flasks *and* big bulging bottles.

I will place upon him the Key of the house of David, Yehsua told Peter I will give thee the Keys to the Kingdom of Heaven and upon this Rock the Gates of Hell shall not prevail. The word Key in Hebrew means Pey Tav Chet, Open door a hole for entering, to engrave, to be marked, the engraving of Eyeh Asher Eyeh or the Mark of the Beast 666.

A door of entering a gate, there is a key to take you from the gates of Hell into the gates of Glory. Mem water, Peh mouth to speak, Tav Cross, Chet Wall, we are going through a wall with our mouth by the Prophetic gifting. To draw a Sword from opening from the sheath, same as key, Parr able means to draw your sword, the Parable is the Key that opens the Glory of the Kingdom. Parr able means two parallel lines which come to a point, which resemblance is a sword. The word is like a two double edge sword. The Apostle ask Yeshua why do you teach in Parables, Yeshua says behold I tell you a mystery, the understanding, knowledge and revelation come by symbolisms and parables by the Leading of the Holy Spirit.

Yeshua is the Head of the church, keys on the shoulders, the shoulders carried the Ark of the Covenant, so in order to carry the Glory you need the Mind of Christ the secrets and Mysteries which hardly no one wants to hear. Proverbs 25:2 *It is* the glory of God to conceal a thing: but the honor of kings *is* to search out a matter. If you're going to be a King, you need to search out this next move, as your mind is changed you will receive your immortal body, be ye renewed by the renewing of your mind. Metamorphosis means to be changed. We are stepping into celebration, think how do you feel, no go back to these other churches, and tell them the end is coming, and looking for caves to hide. Doomsday preferences and kits of fear lol, computer chips and Apocalypse, the Anti-Christ is going to get you fear tactics, most of you are the Antichrist. 1 John 2:27 But you have received the Holy Spirit, and he lives within you, so you don't need anyone to teach you what is true. For the Spirit teaches you everything you need to know, and what he teaches is true--it is not a lie. So just as he has taught you, remain in fellowship with Christ.

So if you do not have the Holy Spirit or the Edification of speaking in Tongues, how do you know what your been taught, or what the secrets or mysteries and understanding of the kingdom is. Psalms 119:105 Your word is a lamp to my feet and a light to my path. So when you receive the Holy Spirit and receive his revelation, he starts filling the lamps within you which are the seven spirits of God. Let me give you clarification of this Saints.

1 John 2:15 Do not love or cherish the world or the things that are in the world. If anyone loves the world, love for the Father is not in him. You notice the word world 3 times.

For all that is in the world—the lust of the flesh [craving for sensual gratification] and the lust of the eyes [greedy longings of the mind] and the pride of life [assurance in one's own resources or in the stability of earthly things]— these do not come from the Father but are from the world [itself]. The word world twice.

And the world passes away and disappears, and with it the forbidden cravings (the passionate desires, the lust) of it; but he who does the will of God and carries out His purposes in his life abides (remains) forever. The world once. Saints the word world came in a form 6times. The mark of the Beast is 666 not the computer chip. The bible speaks of ignorance and carnal mentality.

Boys (lads), it is the last time (hour, the end of this age). And as you have heard that the antichrist [he who will oppose Christ in the guise of Christ] is coming, even now many antichrists have arisen, which confirms our belief that it is the final (the end) time. People who disguise themselves as Christians or any other religion with their false names and gods and idols.

They went out from our number, but they did not [really] belong to us; for if they had been of us, they would have remained with us. But [they withdrew] that it might be plain that they all are not of us. It specifically stated they went out from our number, meaning they were amongst us, they did not belong to us, they would have remained if they were for us, but they left. Who are the Antichrists it's the Carnal Christians and every other religion that opposes these instructions and teachings of the Holy Spirit with His Apostles and Prophets.

Revelation 3;7 And to the angel (messenger) of the assembly (church) in Philadelphia write: These are the words of the Holy One, the True One, He Who has the key of David, Who opens and no one shall shut, Who shuts and no one shall open: I know your [record of] works *and* what you are doing. See! I have set before you a door wide open which no one is able to shut; I know that you have but little power, and yet you have kept My Word *and* guarded My message and have not renounced *or* denied My name. When you Deny His name Yeshua or Yehsua his true name Saints, just as much as you received the False name Jesus Christ, with an open heart you can receive his True Name without ignorance.

Take note! I will make those of the synagogue of Satan who say they are Jews and are not (Those who Teach the Tithe-They are not Levites), but lie—behold, I will make them come and bow down before your feet and learn *and* acknowledge that I have loved you.

He who overcomes (is victorious), I will make him a pillar in the sanctuary of My God; he shall never be put out of it *or* go out of it, and I will write on him the name of My God and the name of the city of My God, the new Jerusalem, which descends from My God out of heaven, and My own new name. Pillar in Hebrew Ammud means *pillar*, supporting house, pillars in a Tabernacle. He shall never be put out of it or go out of it (Immortality Body like From Forever).

He who can hear, let him listen to *and* heed what the Spirit says to the assemblies (churches).17 For you say, I am rich; I have prospered *and* grown wealthy, and I am in need of nothing; and you do not realize *and* understand that you are wretched, pitiable, poor, blind, and naked.

Therefore I counsel you to purchase from Me gold refined *and* tested by fire, that you may be [truly] wealthy, and white clothes to clothe you and to keep the shame of your nudity from being seen, and salve to put on your eyes, that you may see. True wealth is the circumcision of the heart.

Those whom I [dearly and tenderly] love, I tell their faults and convict *and* convince *and* reprove and chasten [I discipline and instruct them]. So be enthusiastic *and* in earnest *and* burning with zeal and repent [changing your mind and attitude]. Prophecy is for correction also saints.

Behold, I stand at the door and knock; if anyone hears *and* listens to *and* heeds My voice and opens the door, I will come in to him and will eat with him, and he [will eat] with Me. Eyeh Asher Eyeh is speaking to the door of your heart.

CHAPTER 6

Let's move on Romans 1:21 Because when they knew *and* recognized Him as God, they did not honor and glorify Him as God or give Him thanks. But instead they became futile *and* godless in their thinking [with vain imaginings, foolish reasoning, and stupid speculations] and their senseless minds were darkened.22 Claiming to be wise, they became fools [professing to be smart, they made simpletons of themselves].

28 And so, since they did not see fit to acknowledge God *or* approve of Him *or* consider Him worth the knowing, God gave them over to a base *and* condemned mind to do things not proper *or* decent *but* loathsome, 29 Until they were filled (permeated and saturated) with every kind of unrighteousness, iniquity, grasping *and* covetous greed, and malice. [They were] full of envy *and* jealousy, murder, strife, deceit *and* treachery, ill will *and* cruel ways. [They were] secret backbiters *and* gossipers.

31 [They were] without understanding, conscienceless *and* faithless, heartless *and* loveless [and] merciless. Let me give you the Revelation and the Definition of the word Christian-Abominable Swine flu lol, about such a great percentage of churches when you ask for money, food, shelter or clothing and they do not consider your needs run out the building as fast as you can and never return. Yes saints by the look of the building you can consider by your own decision if they have the way and means to help you. The bible says Matthew 5:42 Give to the one who begs

from you, and do not refuse the one who would borrow from you.

Here is a short version of the Book of Revelation stating how they think they are Jews or Levites in the church receiving and teaching the misused doctrine or teaching of Tithe. Deuteronomy 14:22 You shall surely tithe all the yield of your seed produced by your field each year. There was many laws regarding the Tithe, which never changed from the Old Testament Covenant Point of view but did change in the New Covenant.

And you shall eat before the Lord your God in the place in which He will cause His Name [and Presence] to dwell the tithe (tenth) of your grain, your new wine, your oil, and the first lings of your herd and your flock that you may learn [reverently] to fear the Lord your God always.

And if the distance is too long for you to carry your tithe, or the place where the Lord your God chooses to set His Name [and Presence] is too far away for you, when the Lord your God has blessed you,

Then you shall turn it into money, and bind up the money in your hand, and shall go to the place [of worship] which the Lord your God has chosen. The first tithe was to the Priest (Levite) Second Tithe was for a granary storehouse.

And you may spend that money for whatever your appetite craves, for oxen, or sheep, or new wine or strong[er] drink, or whatever you desire; and you shall eat there before the Lord your God and you shall rejoice, you and your household. Third tithe Eyeh Asher Eyeh allowed you to keep it. Now what church who practices Tithes tells you,

you can keep your Tithe this month lol, now that was funny you can laugh or are you have possibly been bewitched, well bewitching yourself.

And you shall not forsake *or* neglect the Levite [God's minister] in your towns, for he has been given no share or inheritance with you.

At the end of every three years you shall bring forth all the tithe of your increase the same year and lay it up within your towns. You notice they Tithed three times in one year or every three Years. Saints this is just a short brief description.

And the Levite [because he has no part or inheritance with you] and the stranger *or* temporary resident, and the fatherless and the widow who are in your towns shall come and eat and be satisfied, so that the Lord your God may bless you in all the work of your hands that you do. So it specifically states that the stranger who is not part of your congregation and not a member of your Occult Demonic Fortress lol, temporary resident just visiting the church, you know how they say who are our first time visitors we have some items to give you, a member ship contract to Bewitch you of your money, we need your address, telephone number, email and possibly more information to cast spells on you. The fatherless and the widow that is struggling who are in your towns (Churches) - shall come and eat and be Satisfied) Every single one of you have every God given rights to the Tithe of the church, every Sunday or every time they pick up an offering, they are Commanded By Eyeh Asher Eyeh to Pass out Money, since the Tithe is all money.

Well you might say, if they did that then everyone would come to this church and just come for the money, well of course it says in the word of God it's OK for them to share in the portions of it. Now where in the New Testament or Covenant does it change these rules or regulations not to give or aid, the stranger, temporary resident, the fatherless and the widow. Wow Saints I hope you get the Understanding. Romans 1:31 [They were] without understanding, conscienceless *and* faithless, heartless *and* loveless [and] merciless. 2 Timothy 3:2 For people will love only themselves and their money. They will be boastful and proud, scoffing at God, disobedient to their parents, and ungrateful. They will consider nothing sacred. So who are the Parents and being ungrateful with the money and the people for the positions they have. Scoff in Hebrew means to dismiss (Eyeh Asher Eyeh order and alignment), and as if imitating a foreigner (To mock), to imitate something that once was and is no more.

Saints keep listening here it goes, Ephesians 2:12 [Remember] that you were at that time separated (living apart) from Christ [excluded from all part in Him], utterly estranged *and* outlawed from the rights of Israel as a nation, and strangers with no share in the sacred compacts of the [Messianic] promise [with no knowledge of or right in God's agreements, His covenants]. And you had no hope (no promise); you were in the world without God. You were once a Foreigner, you were not included in the Promise of the Tithe.

12   But now in Christ Jesus, you who once were [so] far away, through (by, in) the blood of Christ have been brought near. We have been brought near by the Blood of Yeshua and His Holy Sacred Name. Acts 26:12

"Thereupon, as I went to Damascus with authority and commission from the chief priests, 13 at midday, O king, I saw in the way a light from heaven, brighter than the brightness of the sun, shining round about me and those who journeyed with me.14 And when we had all fallen to the earth, I heard a voice speaking unto me, and saying in the Hebrew tongue, 'Saul, Saul, why persecute thoust Me? It is hard for thee to kick against the goads.'15 And I said, 'Who art Thou, Lord?' And He said, 'I am Jesus whom thou persecutest. Wait just a minute Saints the name Jesus is not a Hebrew Name, How come Yeshua name of the Hebrew Dialect was not Administered in the Bible Hello!.

Still Ephesians 2:14 For He is [Himself] our peace (our bond of unity and harmony). He has made us both [Jew and Gentile] one [body], and has broken down (destroyed, abolished) the hostile dividing wall between us, by abolishing in His [own crucified] flesh the enmity [caused by] the Law with its decrees and ordinances [which He annulled]; that He from the two might create in Himself one new man [one new quality of humanity out of the two], so making peace. Tithe was a Law, now when you hear a Demon Spirit Say about the Tithe, well what should you be doing under the grace of God and Jesus Christ. You should be tithing under grace that is a Bewitchment. And [He designed] to reconcile to God both [Jew and Gentile, united] in a single body by means of His cross, thereby killing the mutual enmity *and* bringing the feud to an end.

For it is through Him that we both [whether far off or near] now have an introduction (access) by one [Holy] Spirit to the Father [so that we are able to approach Him]. When you hear the Bewitchment, for those who are Tithers are under Covenant, and you Tithe to this Acknowledgment you have been Bewitched. Ephesians 1:13 In Him you also who have heard the Word of Truth, the glad tidings (Gospel) of your salvation, and have believed in *and* adhered to *and* relied on Him, were stamped with the seal of the long-promised Holy Spirit.14 That [Spirit] is the guarantee of our inheritance [the first fruits(Tithe), the pledge and foretaste, the down payment on our heritage], in anticipation of its full redemption *and* our acquiring [complete] possession of it—to the praise of His glory.

Therefore you are no longer outsiders (exiles, migrants, and aliens, excluded from the rights of citizens), but you now share citizenship with the saints (God's own people, consecrated and set apart for Himself); and you belong to God's [own] household.

You are built upon the foundation of the apostles and prophets with Christ Jesus Himself the chief Cornerstone. So who are the Nurturing Head Parents in the body, Spiritual fathers and mothers, his Apostles and Prophets? They will not considered anything Sacred, they are ungrateful. The offering of money is considered sacred, it is to be place at the feet of the Apostles and Prophets (Parents who are in charge) working together with the Fivefold Ministry. The ones Ungrateful they have made a decision to Mock Gods Alignment and Order, to be in control of the Money and the People's Hearts, body, mind, soul and spirit.

OK Saints let's move on, John 10: 10 "Verily, verily I say unto you, he that entereth not by the door into the sheepfold, but climbeth up some other way, the same is a thief and a robber.2 But he that entereth in by the door is the shepherd of the sheep.3 To him the doorkeeper openeth, and the sheep hear his voice; and he calleth his own sheep by name and leadeth them out. Saints to those who have the Key which is the secrets and mysteries of revelations of understanding of the Parables have the Key. Those who do not have it or considered thieves and robbers taking what they will and can or cause chaos.

4 And when he putted forth his own sheep, he goeth before them and the sheep follow him, for they know his voice.5 And a stranger will they not follow, but will flee from him, for they know not the voice of strangers."7 Then said Jesus unto them again, "Verily, verily I say unto you, I am the door of the sheep.8 All that ever came before Me are thieves and robbers, but the sheep did not hear them.

False sheep hear false teachings or they need to untwist the teachings of religious doctrine to come out, which is stubbornness and ignorance. 9 I am the door; by Me if any man enter in, he shall be saved, and shall go in and out, and find pasture. Come eat, go out and find pastures, come in and out with the key you have cause you understand to hear his voice.

13   But he that is a hireling (Someone who is working for Money) and not the shepherd, whose own the sheep are not, see the wolf coming and he sheep and fleeth; and the wolf catcheth them and scattereth sheep. Your seed is your money, send your seed of money and watch what God does for you, The Spirit of Bacchus, Thyrsus and Hedonism- As a theory of value, hedonism states that all and only pleasure is intrinsically valuable and all and only

pain is intrinsically not valuable. 13 The hireling fleeth because he is a hireling (Works for Money and Tithe), and careth not for the sheep. Stealing or Thief means kleptomaniac-slaughter the sheep to sacrifice them with their false teachings, they can't help themselves to steal the word, steal or stop or shut up the revelations, refrain those to get a hold of the keys of the kingdom.

Psalms 58:4 Their poison *is* like the poison of a serpent: *they are* like the deaf adder *that* stoppeth her ear. Venomous Poison-ness snakes, they do what lay eggs, how prophetically, it's called false teachings and false impregnation when you receive these eggs in your spirit you begin to Die Physically and Spiritually. Appollumi in Hebrew- means to destroy you, to kill you by their false teachings and send you straight to Hell, Appo means be separated, Ilumi means enlightened, they have been superheated by the light. . An **apocalypse-meaning 'un-covering' a lifting of the veil or revelation in Wikipedia online Saints.** The Spirit of Appollyn that comes from the Bottomless pit in the book of Revelation, comes and takes away a false church and those who do not want to be enlightened.

Matt 16:19 "I will give you the keys of the kingdom of heaven; whatever you bind on earth will be bound in heaven, and whatever you loose on earth will be loosed in heaven." Saints more Understanding of what Keys mean, Luke 11:52 "Woe to you experts in the law, because you have taken away the key to knowledge. You yourselves have not entered, and you have hindered those who were entering." Most congregations are taught by thieves and have no clue to what they are receiving.

CHAPTER 7

Let's move on Saints, Shut up in Hebrew satham-*stop up* springs of water, in sense of *shut out*, shut ears against, *shut up, keep close*, prophetic words. When Yeshua releases the rain of revelation, it means he is releasing his compassion on you. When you reject Yahweh revelation, you reject Gods compassion, compassion will be inexpressible towards you God will have no pity on you for this last move here on earth. Saints like I clarified before yes I'm not implying to be all superstitious and spiritual, yes you can receive revelation and understanding through experiences supernaturally, speaking in tongues(without hiding), seeking Eyeh Asher Eyeh face to face, and worshiping him whole heartedly. Saints all you have to do is Confess, 1 John 1:9 If we confess our sins, he is faithful and just to forgive us *our* sins, and to cleanse us from all unrighteousness. This is the ultimate answer, let him know I don't understand but I am willing to do thy will, help me I'm a hot mess, I need your aid and help.

Matthew 16:19 19 I will give you the keys of the kingdom of heaven; and whatever you bind (declare to be improper and unlawful) on earth [a]must be what is already bound in heaven; and whatever you lose (declare lawful) on earth [b]must be what is already loosed in heaven.

The Father is talking about releasing the secrets and mysteries of the kingdom, he is not talking about binding up demons, when to shut it off and when to release it. Matthew 7:6 Give not that which is holy unto the dogs, neither cast your pearls before the swine, lest haply they trample them under their feet, and turn and rend you.

Rend in Hebrew Qara-*tear* away or out: veils, shredding them like there worth nothing, to slander you. Luke 11:52 52 Woe to you, lawyers (experts in the Mosaic Law)! For you have taken away the key to knowledge; you did not go in yourselves, and you hindered *and* prevented those who were entering. Revelation 3:7 And to the angel of the church in Philadelphia write: These things saith he that is holy, he that is true, he that hath the key of David, he that openeth and none shall shut, and that shutteth and none openeth: This scripture is talking about the keys of the releasing of the secrets of his revelations of his word, it is Yeshua who has the keys. James 5:7 Be patient therefore, brethren, until the coming of the Lord. Behold, the husbandman waiteth for the precious fruit of the earth, being patient over it, until it receive the early and latter rain. The fruits are the seeds being planted by the Apostles and Prophets treading out the grain and given it out as food manna, both the early and latter rain. Giving you seeds to be impregnated by the word of revelation preparing for the Bridegroom, to give birth to the Apostolic God Head within you. The seed is the word, the seed that goes in the ground earth you, when the earth manifests the seed, which then Harvest the grain(Former Rain), animals(Beasts of the Earth-Carnality) then Fruits (The Latter Rain). Now when the fruits come forth you bring an offering which also resembles a sacrifice unto Eyeh Asher Eyeh.

So you offer up an offering of yourselves as the good fruit, you are caught up, you go up into smoke, when you move into his presence of Eyeh Asher Eyeh caught up in the heavens in a Realm up Glory he covers your sins and protects you. This is a place and the Realm of his Glory that the enemy cannot enter in. There is no room for Spiritual

Warfare, There is complete Confidence in the Holy Spirit doing the job. So when you become Smoke you're a sweet smell to his Nostrils, filled with Revelation, then what does a cloud do it rains, so then you can become a light unto the world. You will have the ability when to bring it out or shut up the heavens within you by the leading of the Holy Spirit. You become the Pillar and the Cloud of His Shekina Glory.

You then become the dew unto this earth, you also begin to pour out what has been giving to you. Genesis 27:28 May God give you heaven's dew and earth's richness-- an abundance of grain and new wine. What fragrance are you to the father Isaiah 65:5Yet they say to each other, 'Don't come too close or you will defile me! I am holier than you!' These people are a stench in my nostrils, an acrid smell that never goes away.

Isaiah 1:13-13 The incense you bring me is a stench in my nostrils! Your celebrations of the new moon and the Sabbath day, and your special days for fasting -- even your most pious meetings -- are all sinful and false. I want nothing more to do with them. 14 I hate all your festivals and sacrifices. I cannot stand the sight of them! 15 From now on, when you lift up your hands in prayer, I will refuse to look. Even though you offer many prayers, I will not listen. For your hands are covered with the blood of your innocent victims. 16 Wash yourselves and be clean! Let me no longer see your evil deeds. Give up your wicked ways. 17 Learn to do good. Seek justice. Help the oppressed. Defend the orphan. Fight for the rights of widows. 18 "Come now, let us argue this out," says the LORD. "No matter how deep the stain of your sins, I can remove it. I can make you as clean as freshly fallen snow. Even if you are stained as red as crimson, I can make you as white as wool. 19 If you will only obey me and let me help you, then you will have plenty to eat. 20 But if you keep turning away and refusing to listen, you will be destroyed by your enemies. I, the LORD, have spoken!" 21 See how Jerusalem, once so faithful, has become a prostitute. Once the home of justice and righteousness, she is now filled with murderers. 22 Once like pure silver, you have become like worthless slag. Once so pure, you are now like watered-down wine. 23 Your leaders are rebels, the companions of thieves. All of them take bribes and refuse to defend the orphans and the widows.

Galatians 3:16 Now to Abraham and his seed were the promises made. He saith not, and to seeds, as of many; but as of one, and to thy seed, which is Christ. The Seed is Christ not money. Seed in Hebrew means to sow and to scatter seed, yes but also states to conceive seed to give birth. What sort of seeds are you giving birth to, are you sowing seeds of mercy, grace, favor, love, forgiveness constantly etc.

Money doesn't conceive and give birth to anything. I believe the sowing has to do mostly out of the Adoration of the motive and intentions of the Heart. Also I do believe when a Prophet or Apostle hears from God about sowing a seed it is honored because it's an Apostle or Prophet, it's in a divine rank and order. All I'm saying is test the spirits when there are talking about sowing a seed when it comes to money. I believe the father wants us to sow seeds of righteousness more than anything.

Hosea 10:12 I said, 'Plant the good seeds of righteousness, and you will harvest a crop of love. Plow up the hard ground of your hearts, for now is the time to seek the LORD, that he may come and shower righteousness upon you. James 3:18 and the fruit of righteousness is sown in peace of them that make peace. Yeshua is speaking about the attributes of righteousness being sown to receive back from the father.

About The Author

Hello family, I'm just going to give you a brief illustration of my testimony about me and my life In Yahshua. I'm currently divorced over 10 years one daughter, my daughter is 13 one of the greatest life's experiences in my life. My parents are Ministers of the good news for the last 45years experience in the prophetic call and commission. My father's an Apostle and my mother's a Prophetess, who's been used for 17 years. I've been trained under the Holy Spirit and will always be in training, ever since my walk I've been taught to die to self and to lay down my own self will for the sake of the Kingdom for transformation. My biological father left me when I was 11, I had an encounter with God himself, the Father when I was 18 years of age.

One day everyone was gone, my mother had three children I am the middle child, it was around midnight walking around my home. I spoke to myself and stated I was all alone then the phone rang it was weird, then I said hello the voice said" Are you alone" I then said who is this. The voice continued and said "This is your Father, your not alone." Then I said, "ok who is this, stop playing around!" The voice continued and said, "Go to the mirror and then stated are you alone?" Then I said, "Who is this the voice?" Then he continued, "This is your Father in Heaven." I was stunned for that moment and couldn't grasp or understand the situation and my brain went blank.

Since that day, I've been divorced ten years, slept in the streets homeless for about 6 years, kicked out of churches for being too prophetic, slept in houses with ministers who are apostles and prophets that astro projected out of their bodies.

While I have disobeyed Yahweh several times, he allowed me to see the demonic realm and was attacked heavily by my own disobedience, also by other leaders that have mastered the gift inside them using for their own self gain. Trained under the gift of the discerning of spirits, to discern the motive and intents of the hearts of the people around me.

I was just recently pulled out from being homeless, several years ago about 2 ½ to be precise, generational curses broken off from biological father who made a deal with Satan, An apostle prophesied and stated your biological father made a deal with Satan to have the blood of two of his children for promise for money for the rest of his life. My sister was cured from whooping cough there was no cure at that time. I was set free from several demonic spirits that are so real. My walk in ministry was to discern why so much division, only by Yahshua's grace and the Holy Spirit has graced me to understand the spirit of influence & religion using venom of false doctrine and false prophecies that's been impregnated in the hearts of gods children & have been left crippled and shuts down their own immune system.

My present state I'm ordained minister, my belief is to be a life living sacrifice for Yahweh's kingdom , only to be servant to others and help one another reach Yahweh's purpose n destiny in our lives. To unveil the mysteries and revelations of this kingdom age for all his children to be set free from religion, jezebel spirits, spirit of influence, psychology, false hope (false prophesies), rejection, abandonment guilt, shame, control, seared conscious, subconscious, conscious, mesmoratic cells, trauma, familiar spirits, camellia spirits that transforms and changes color, cockatrice spirit, the false god of Prosperity, Fortune & Destiny, mystical influences that general spirits have had dominion over us.

Isaiah 26: 13-14 (AMP) says, "O Lord, our God, other masters besides You have ruled over us, but we will acknowledge *and* mention Your name only.[14] They [the former tyrant masters] are dead, they shall not live *and* reappear; they are powerless ghosts, they shall not rise *and* come back. Therefore You have visited and made an end of them and caused every memory of them [every trace of their supremacy] to perish." This reference speaks of general demonic spirits even with all religious practices, he will even wipe away the memory of them out of us.

Anthony Montoya

ANTHONY MONTOYA

BOOKS BY ANTHONY MONTOYA

The Seed Of Resurrection

The Fruits Of Favor And Increase

Apocalypse Encrypted! Revelation Unleashed!

Apocalypse Encrypted! Revelation Unleashed! – 2

MINISTRY CONTACT INFORMATION

You may contact Anthony Montoya

through the following sources:

Email Address:

Judah1231@yahoo.com

Website:

anthonymontoyas1.weebly.com